Cheffy Skills Quickies Cookbook
© Mel Alafaci 2023

First printed December 2023 by Ingram Spark

All rights reserved. Except as permitted under the Australian Copyright Act 1968 (for example, a fair dealing for the purposes of study, research, criticism or review), no part of this book may be reproduced, stored in a retrieval system, communicated or transmitted in any form or by any means without prior written permission.

Creator: Mel Alafaci (Author)
Title: Cheffy Skills Quickies Cookbook
ISBN: 9780645808452 (Paperback)
Subjects: Cook Book

Typesetting by Chloe Reynolds - Social Chloe

Chef Mel is taking on the WORLD!

With a smile that can light up a room, Chef Mel Alafaci has become a globally recognised chef and food educator. Her recent success in the USA means she's Australia's hottest rising culinary personality. Born in Zimbabwe, Chef Mel lived in South Africa before moving to Australia and starting her reign in the global foodie market.

She has an unwavering passion for cooking, eating, and teaching. And her intoxicating enthusiasm, authenticity, and unique culinary lingo will have you hungry to flex your muscles in the kitchen. Chef Mel is brilliant at adding humour, shortcuts, tricks, and hacks to all those tedious tasks, as well as making the scary ones simple and easy to accomplish.

CHEF MEL THE HAPPY CHEF | **@CHEFMEL_HAPPYCHEF** | **WWW.CHEFMEL.ME**

ABOUT MEL

Mel Alafaci has been passionate about food her whole life. She's the founder of Vanilla Zulu Cooking School, one of Australia's leading cooking schools, and has more than 28 years of professional cooking experience.

People battle to say her surname... so to make it easy she calls herself CHEF MEL.

WILD ABOUT FOOD!

Recipes

Recipes

Breads, Wraps & Biscuits

2	Quickie Carb-Free Bread in a Mug
3	5-Minute Keto Bread
4	Versatile Bread Recipe/Grissini Sticks
5	Salt & Rosemary Focaccia
6	Pita Bread with Petals & Bling
8	Ciabatta (No Knead, High Hydration, Stretch & Fold Dough)
10	Decadent Brioche
11	Croissants with Cheese or Chocolate
13	Vanilla Glazed Donuts
14	Seeded Wholemeal Wraps
15	Bespoke Culinary Bark AKA Water Crackers
16	Seed Crackers

Pastries

18	Puff Pastry (Pâte Feuilletée)
19	Rough Puff Pastry
20	French Short Crust (Pâte Brisée)
21	Shortest Short Crust (Pâte Sucrée)
23	Phyllo Pastry
24	Choux Pastry
25	Choux Au Craqelin
26	Cream Cheese Pastry
26	Tempura Batter
28	Basic Batter
28	Yorkshire Puddings
29	Basic Scones
30	Sweet Options for Scones
31	Spiced Caramel Fig Rusks with Pistachio

Pasta, Pizza & Gnocchi

33	Basic Pasta Recipe
34	Roasted Pumpkin & Speck Ravioli with Burnt Sage Butter
36	Roasted Spinach & Ricotta Ravioli with Burnt Sage & Pine Nut Butter
38	Change your Life Bolognaise
40	Authentic Pizza
42	Rustic Italian Gnocchi with Burnt Sage Butter & Pancetta Bark
43	Parmesan Gnocchi Roman Style

Recipes

Soups & Salads

45	Thai Lime, Pea & Coconut Soup with Chilli & Shallot Bling
46	Almond & Chorizo Gazpacho
47	Roast Cauliflower Soup
49	Thai Green Papaya Salad
51	Thai Grilled Beef Salad
52	Kipfler Potato Salad

Egg Dishes

55	How to Poach an Egg
57	Eggs Benedict
59	Easy Omelette
61	Happy Sexy Quickie Eggs

Starters

64	Around the world with a Baked Brie Fondue
65	Fragrant Spring Garlic & Tarragon Brie
66	Butternut & Feta Hummus
68	Tarragon Scented Paté with Shiraz & Strawberry Jelly
70	Tarragon Scented Paté served with Crostini
71	Duck & Pork Terrine with Cranberries & Pistachios
72	Chicken & Porcini Quenelle with Parmesan Black Pepper Cream Sauce
73	Chorizo & Sweet Potato Croquettes
75	Easy Cheese Soufflés
76	Glamourous Chicken & Cream Cheese Balls
78	Thai Fish Cakes
79	Beef Carpaccio
80	Rosemary Scented Egg Yolk Confit
81	Steak Tartare
83	Crispy Pork Spring Rolls
85	Scented Beef & Basil Spring Rolls

Mains

88	Mince with Pistachio & Date Gravel
90	Moroccan Scented Mini Meat Loves with Cucumber & Cumin Sauce
92	Sexy Stir Fries
94	Delectable Braised Duck with Spiced Carrot Purée
95	Twice Cooked Sticky Plum & Ginger Pork Rashers
97	Braised Pork Belly served on Caramelised Pear & Onion

Recipes

Lamb Dishes

99	Lamb Backstrap with Pistachio Gravel
100	Fragrant Leg of Lamb with Turmeric & Cumin Rub
102	Fragrant Lamb Shoulder with Sticky Date, Pistachio & Lemon Gravel

Steak Dishes

104	How to Cook the Perfect Steak
105	Steak Done-ness Test
106	Sous Vide Sexy Black Steak with Juniper & Black Salt Rub
107	Fillet with Porcini & Sage Cream

Seafood Dishes

110	Creamy Sherry & Garlic Mussels
110	Scampi/Prawns Poached in Burnt Almond & Sage Butter
112	Snapper Baked with Nam Jim or Chiang Mai
114	Seared Crispy Skin Fish with Pancetta Bark & Rustic Pea Mash
116	Giant Tiger Prawns with Peri Peri
117	Tea Smoked Crispy Skin Salmon
118	Spectacular Paella Made Easy

Chicken Dishes

121	Sage, Sweet Potato & Speck Hot Rubbed Spatchcock with Spray Tan
122	Tarragon & Porcini Stuffed Spatchcock
123	Tea Poached Asian Spatchcock with Fresh, Hot & Sexy Salad
124	Coq Au Vin Featuring Spatchcock served with Fragrant Mash.
126	Home Smoked Chicken Mayo & Mint Gourmet Stacks

Vegetable Dishes

128	Cauliflower Paella
129	Truffled Mushroom Pizza with Cauliflower Sweet Potato Topping
131	Sexy Roast Vegetables
132	Gourmet Sweet Potato & Cauliflower Mash
132	Quick Sweet Potato Curry
133	Sexy Petit Pois

The Art of Making Stock

135	Chicken Stock
135	Simple Beef/Bone Stock

Recipes

Basic Sauces

139	**CLASSIC BÉCHAMEL/VELOUTÉ**
140	*Daughter Sauces of Béchamel & Velouté:*
140	• Sauce Allemande AKA Sauce Parisienne
140	• Sauce Aurore
141	• Caper Sauce
141	• Sauce Chaudfroid
141	• Egg Sauce
141	• Sauce a'la' Estragon/Tarragon Sauce
142	• Sauce Mornay
142	• Mushroom sauce
142	• Sauce Soubise
142	• Sauce Supreme
143	Brown Sauce/Demi-Glace
144	*Daughter Sauces of Brown Sauce:*
144	• Sauce Chasseur
144	• Sauce Duxelles
144	• Sauce Madère/Madeira Sauce
145	House Made BBQ Sauce
146	Sugo Sauce with Roasted Capsicum

Hot Emulsified Sauces

147	Sauce Beurre Blanc
147	Sauce Blanche au Beurre (White Sauce enriched with butter)
148	**HOLLANDAISE SAUCE**
149	Blender Hollandaise Sauce
150	Burnt Butter Hollandaise/Sauce Noisette
151	*Daughter Sauces of Hollandaise Sauce*
151	• Béarnaise Sauce
151	• Sauce Choron
151	• Sauce Maltaise
152	• Sauce Mireille
152	• Sauce Moutarde
153	Parmesan Pepper Cream Sauce
154	Truffled Cream Sauce
155	Fragrant Mushroom Duxelles

Cold Emulsified Sauces

156	**CLASSIC MAYONNAISE**
157	• Porcini Black Salt Mayonnaise
158	• Lemon Pepper Mayonnaise
159	*Mayonnaise Daughter Dressings*
159	• Caesar Dressing
159	• Ranch Dressing

Recipes

Dips & Dressings

161	Beetroot, Balsamic & Rosemary Sweet Drizzling Sauce
161	Tumeric Spiced Concasse
162	House-made Sweet Chilli Sauce
162	Basic Thai Salad Dressing
163	Vietnamese Dipping Sauce
163	Carrot Ginger Dressing
164	Chermoula
166	Chimichurri

Butters

168	Whipped Truffle or Porcini Butter
169	Turmeric, Chilli & Lime Butter with Black Crust
171	Clarified Butter
172	Herbed Burnt Basil & Black Pepper Butter

Purées & Pastes

174	Sexy Lemon Pea Purée
175	Fragrant Turmeric Scented Gourmet Ceci Mash
176	Spiced Carrot Purée
178	Delicious Yellow Butterbean Purée
179	Chiang Mai Curry Paste
179	Massaman Curry Paste

Desserts

182	Blueberry Pancakes
184	Crepe Citronelle
185	Cannoli
186	Pastry Cream - Crème Patissiere
187	Delicious Versatile Nougat
188	Pistachio Lemon Butter Cookies
189	Vanilla Apple Lattice Pie
190	Easy Crumble
191	Champagne & Rose Water Jellies Scented with Orange Zest
192	Brulé with Famous Tappy Tap Sugar
194	Baked Sweet Soufflés
195	Cold Lemon or Passionfruit Soufflé
196	Pear & Ricotta Tarts
198	Catalan Custard Tarts
199	Lime & Palm Sugar Creams with Famous Tappy Tap Sugar
200	Sexy Honeycomb for Dessert Bling
201	Spun Sugar
202	Blood Orange & Lemon Curd

Recipes

Ice Cream, Gelato & Sorbet

- 205 — Bruleé scented Ice Cream with Nutted Caramel Shards
- 206 — Gelato - you choose your flavour!
- 207 — Burnt Pear Butter Gelato
- 208 — Vanilla Ice Cream with Salted Pistachio Toffee
- 209 — Lime & Coconut Ice Cream
- 210 — Bruleé Scented Semi Freddo with Tappy Tap Sugar
- 211 — House-Made Ice Cream Cone or Basket
- 212 — Spiced Milk Sorbet
- 213 — Lime & Coconut Panna Cotta
- 215 — Vanilla Panna Cotta

Chocolate

- 218 — Gourmet Chocolate Tarts
- 219 — Death by Chocolate Marshamallow Ice Cream using Paté a Bombe
- 221 — Death by Chocolate Platter featuring 'Spiced' Death by Chocolate Brownies
- 222 — Chocolate Ganache
- 223 — Complexion-Busting Chocolate Salami
- 224 — Death by Chocolate Complexion Busting Pistachio Rocky Road
- 225 — Chocolate Bark or Tiles
- 226 — Dessert Dust

Delectable Foams

- 228 — Beetroot & Rosemary Foam (savoury)
- 228 — Lime & Cilantro Foam (savoury)
- 228 — Strawberry, Lemon & Basil Foam (sweet)

Breads, Wraps & Biscuits

Happiness is... the smell of freshly baked bread.
Breadmaking will depend on the temperature of your kitchen. If it's a warm summer's day, we could only wait 10 minutes for the dough to prove or double, but on a cold winter's day, you could wait an hour, so find a warm spot in your house, and it will become your bread-making spot!

Quickie Carb-Free Bread in a Mug

SERVINGS: 1

INGREDIENTS

1 heaped tablespoon crunchy or smooth peanut butter
1 egg
1/4 teaspoon baking powder
1 straight-sided coffee mug
Cooking spray

METHOD

Mix the peanut butter, egg and baking powder together by smashing them against the side of a small bowl with the back of a tablespoon. You will have to keep scooping the paste back in to bring it together. The thick peanut paste will take a bit of squishing to blend with the egg and powder, but keep going!

Now put this batter into a greased coffee mug and cook in your microwave for ONE MINUTE.

Cool and then slice and have on its own with your favourite spread, or as part of another dish.

Too easy. Too cheap. Too brilliant.

5-Minute Keto Bread

SERVINGS: 8 SLICES

INGREDIENTS

200ml water
200g almond meal
40g flax seeds *or chia seeds or LSA mix*
40g coconut flour
4 eggs
50g coconut oil or melted butter
1 teaspoon baking powder
1/2 teaspoon bicarb
1 teaspoon apple cider vinegar

METHOD

Simply place all these ingredients into a blender and blitz a few times until you have a smooth paste. Place into a greased baking dish and then bake at 180C for 15-25 minutes, depending on the size of your container. I use two small pie dishes, and then my cooking time is 20 minutes, but you'll have to adjust depending on the size of your dish.
Once cooked, allow it to cool and then you MUST store it in the fridge to extend its life.
I slice mine when cold, and then all I have to do is pop into the toaster to refresh.

Enjoy and please let me know what you think of this amazing carb-free bread.

Happy Cooking

Versatile Bread Recipe/Grissini Sticks

SERVINGS: 8-10

INGREDIENTS

450 g plain or baker's flour
2 teaspoons instant yeast
320 ml lukewarm water
2 teaspoons extra flour
2 teaspoons sugar
30ml oil
1 teaspoon salt

METHOD

Add the yeast to the warm water, with the 2 teaspoons extra flour and sugar, stir and set aside for about 10 minutes until foamy. Now mix this liquid with the flour, salt, and oil and bring it together until it forms a smooth dough.

Place on a floured surface and knead until the dough is smooth and pliable. By hand, at least 6 minutes. Use your mixer and a dough hook if you aren't doing this by hand, about 5-7 minutes at least.

Now place the dough into a greased bowl and, cover it with a clean wet cloth, and allow to prove for about 20 minutes or until doubled in size. Remove from the bowl and shape as required on a floured surface. **(For grissini, take tablespoon size balls and roll them into long, thin 'stick's. Place on a baking tray and prove for 20 minutes before baking.)**

Top and shape with ingredients of your choice. Now allow to prove for a second time for about 30 minutes in its shape and then bake in a pre-heated oven of 180 c for about 15 minutes until golden.

TO SERVE: Pour 2 tablespoons of extra virgin olive oil onto a saucer or side plate, and pour a tablespoon of balsamic vinegar in the middle of the plate. Delicious.

Salt & Rosemary Focaccia

SERVINGS: 6-8

INGREDIENTS

DOUGH
- 450 g plain or baker's flour
- 2 teaspoons instant yeast
- 2 teaspoons sugar
- 320 ml lukewarm water,
- 1 teaspoon salt
- 30ml oil
- 2 teaspoons extra flour
- 2 tablespoons polenta or semolina *to give a nice crunchy base*
- Cooking spray to grease the baking tray

TOPPINGS
- 1/2 teaspoon black flake salt or other flake salt
- 1 tablespoon finely chopped Rosemary *chopped finely into a 'gravel'*
- 3 large lashings of extra virgin olive oil

METHOD

Add the yeast to the warm water, with the 2 teaspoons extra flour and sugar, stir and set aside for about 10 minutes until foamy. Now mix this liquid with the flour, salt and oil until it forms a smooth dough. Place on a floured surface and knead until the dough is smooth and pliable. Use your mixer and a dough hook if you aren't doing this by hand, about 5-7 minutes at least!

Now place the dough ball onto a baking sheet that has been greased and dusted with 2 tablespoons of polenta or semolina. Oil the dough ball with some olive oil so it doesn't dry out, and now leave it to prove for 20 minutes. After 20 minutes, hand stretch using the palms of your hands that have been oiled and push the dough to the edges of the baking tray. Make deep holes (Nona's fingerprints) by using your fingertips to poke the dough. Garnish with the sexy black salt flakes, rosemary gravel and oil. Now allow to prove for a second time for about 10 minutes in its shape, and then bake in a preheated oven of 180 c for about 15 minutes until golden.

TO SERVE

Pour 2 tablespoons of extra virgin olive oil onto a saucer or side plate, and pour a tablespoon of balsamic vinegar in the middle of the plate.

Pita Bread with Petals & Bling

SERVINGS: 6-8

INGREDIENTS

450 g plain or baker's flour

1 tablespoon instant dried yeast

320 ml lukewarm water

2 teaspoons salt

2 teaspoons sugar

30ml oil

2 teaspoons extra flour

1 teaspoon black seeds, poppy, nigella, black basil

1 tablespoon marigold petals (or other edible petals) optional

1 teaspoon turmeric (optional)

METHOD

Add the yeast to the warm water, with the 2 teaspoons extra flour and sugar, stir and set aside for about 10 minutes until foamy. Now mix this liquid with the flour, seeds, salt, oil, petals and bling, and bring together until it forms a smooth dough.

Place on a floured surface and knead until the dough is smooth and pliable.

Use your mixer and a dough hook if you aren't doing this by hand, about 5-7 minutes at least!

Now place the dough into a greased bowl and cover it with a clean wet cloth, and allow to prove for about 15 minutes or until doubled in size. Remove from the bowl and shape as required on a floured surface. Top and shape with ingredients of your choice.

Now allow to prove for a second time for about 10 minutes in its shape, and then bake in a preheated oven of 180 c for about 15 minutes until golden OR you can cook these in a hot, dry, empty pan, a few minutes on each side.

Ciabatta (No Knead Stretch & Fold Dough)

Ciabatta
(No Knead, High Hydration, Stretch & Fold Dough)

SERVINGS: 8-12

INGREDIENTS

350g baker's flour
1 heaped teaspoon of instant yeast
280ml hand hot water (not cold or swearword hot)
1 flat teaspoon salt
30ml/2 tablespoons olive oil
1 tablespoon chopped rosemary
1/4 cup chopped olives (optional)

METHOD

This is super easy; you are going to just love this dough.
Please watch my full demo on my YOUTUBE channel.

Add all the ingredients into a large bowl and use a strong spoon to bring it together. Once mixed nicely, it will look a lot wetter than a standard bread dough, cover with a wet cloth and then allow to prove for 10 minutes. After ten minutes, you should see some yeast bubble activity. Dip your hand in water from a tap or bowl, and then when your hand is wet, dig down along the side of the bowl under the dough and then scoop and stretch the dough to the top and centre.

Repeat this stretch and fold method about 8 times, turning the bowl as you go; keep wetting your hand so that the dough doesn't stick to you. Prove again for a further 10 minutes, repeat the stretch and fold and then prove and stretch and fold for a third and final time. The dough is now ready to be shaped, so turn it out onto a floured surface. It's a bit tricky to handle, but cut it into two smaller breads or leave it as one large one, depending on what you want and how long you have to cook this. Two smaller breads are faster than one large loaf.

Simply fold the dough over itself, shape it into an oblong or round and place it on a greased and floured baking tray. Sprinkle with about half a teaspoon of flour and then allow to prove for 10 more minutes in it's new shape. Bake, hot and fast, at about 190c for 15 minutes; remove from the oven, wet your hand and flick the crust with a sprinkle of water, and then bake further for approximately 5-8 minutes until nice and crunchy and brown. The water flicking helps create that spectacular crust we get on baguettes and artisan loaves; it's very cool to know how to do this. To test the bread, flick it with your fingers, it should sound hollow and should be gorgeous and brown.

Allow to cool and then cut, serve and enjoy!

Decadent Brioche

Decadent Brioche

SERVINGS: 10-12

BRIOCHE IS AN ENRICHED BREAD DOUGH

INGREDIENTS

450g bakers flour
5ml salt
7g instant yeast
2 eggs
30g sugar
1 teaspoon vanilla (optional)
120 ml warm milk
80ml warm water
120g soft butter
1 egg beaten with some water for the glaze (egg wash)

METHOD

Brioche are enriched bread dough. Place the yeast into the warm milk and water, with the sugar and one teaspoon of the flour. Stir and set aside and allow the yeast to 'sponge'. This is when it starts to foam and will take about 5-15 minutes, depending on how warm the room is. This is just to ensure the yeast is active; it can be added directly into the other ingredients, though, if you know the yeast is fresh.

Now, mix all ingredients, including your sponged yeast liquid, together to form a soft dough. I use a strong spoon to bring it together, and then put it on a floured surface and knead, using flour to prevent the dough from sticking to your hands until the dough is soft and pliable. At least 5-7 minutes. **You can use your stand mixer and dough hook and knead using your machine.** Grease a clean bag and allow the dough to double in size; this will depend on the weather, of course, so cut it open to see if there are adequate air bubbles.

Once proved, divide into equal portions and then divide each dough ball into two balls, one smaller than the other. Place the larger ball on a greased baking sheet or brioche tin and top it with the smaller ball. **Or just make the shape you require.** In this photo I have plaited the loaf. Glaze with the egg wash and set aside to double in size before baking in a moderate oven of 180c for about 15-20 minutes, depending on the size you have made them.

Enjoy.

Croissants with Cheese or Chocolate

**SERVINGS: MAKES 8-12 CROISSANTS
DEPENDING ON SIZE**

INGREDIENTS

360g bakers flour

half teaspoon salt

25g butter

2 teaspoons instant yeast

1-teaspoon sugar

250ml warm water

1 egg

ADDITIONAL INGREDIENTS

180g butter (cut off the block with a sharp knife about 1 cm thick only)

Either 80 g grated cheddar OR 80g chocolate paste for fillings

METHOD

You can either do a sweet or savoury filling...beware. These are addictive. Croissants are an enriched bread dough.

Mix the warm water with the yeast, sugar and a teaspoon of the flour. Do NOT add salt to this mixture!
In a bowl, rub the butter into the flour, add the salt and then add the yeasty water and the egg.
Mix with a strong spoon to form a soft, pliable dough. Dust a surface with a little bit of extra flour and then knead the dough for at least 5 -8 minutes until springy, elastic, and firm; use flour to prevent the dough from sticking to your hands or to the bench, but don't add that much flour that you try the mixture out! The softer the dough, the better the dough!

Place the dough into a greased bowl and cover it with a clean, wet cloth; chill in the fridge for about 10-15 minutes. Now roll out into a rectangle about A4 size, making sure your bench, and your hands and rolling pin are dusted with flour. Any dough sticking to anything can be stressful; flour is your friend; use it to stop your dough from sticking.

Pack the cut butter blocks onto one-third of the dough; you will need to mould it into a rectangle with a spatula or butter knife. Leave a little margin free around the butter of the dough. Now fold the plain pastry over the butter and then the third part over to seal in the butter completely. Press down to seal the butter into its dough and then roll out to the A4 size again. This will roll the butter out into a nice thin layer and roll gently and respectfully so that the butter does not ooze and break through the dough. Be gentle and firm, and also be neat!
Once the pastry is now at A4 size, divide and fold into thirds again and then roll out AGAIN. Do this 3 more times, and you are creating layers within the dough of the butter.

You will need to chill the dough in between rolling so that the pastry is always cool and the butter NEVER pokes or bleeds through the dough. Your dough will behave differently in summer and winter; remember, the yeast is active, and if it gets too warm, the dough will become difficult to handle, so use your fridge to chill it down.

On the last roll, wrap in cling film and let rest in the fridge for 20 minutes. Now roll out into a larger, thinner rectangle, about 60cm x 30 cm. Trim the edges and then cut in half lengthwise.

Cut each strip into long, thin triangles, about 30cm L x 10cm W (large) or 15cm L x 6 W (small)
Take one of the triangles and put the wider edge closest to you with the point pointing away from you. Add either 1 teaspoon grated cheese or 1 teaspoon chocolate ganache (chocolate paste with cream so it doesn't set too hard).

Roll the filling neatly into the triangle, sealing it into the croissant. Curve the croissant into a crescent shape and glaze with egg wash or cream.

Place on a greased baking sheet and then cover with cling film and allow to prove for about 10-30 minutes until doubled in size and puffy. This time will depend on the temperature in your kitchen; of course, if you have a dough-proving function in your fancy oven, you can pop them in there for 20 minutes. I prefer to prove in the fridge for about an hour. Only prove at room temperature if you are in a hurry. Bake in a pre-heated oven of 180c for about 15-20 minutes until golden and brown.

Vanilla Glazed Donuts

SERVINGS: 8-12

INGREDIENTS

450g baker's flour	5ml salt
2 egg yolks	80g sugar
160ml warm milk	100 ml warm water
2 teaspoons sugar	**VANILLA GLAZE**
2 teaspoons flour to sponge yeast	1 cup icing mixture
1 tablespoon instant yeast (allow to sponge)	2-3 tablespoons hot water to mix to a paste
100g butter, melted	Add slowly and add more as needed
10ml vanilla bean paste/extract	1 teaspoon vanilla paste or extract

METHOD

Doughnuts are an enriched bread dough.

Place the warm milk, warm water, sugar and additional flour with the yeast into a jug or bowl.

Allow to sponge/foam for approximately 10 minutes.

Now add to the remaining ingredients and then mix together with a strong spoon.

Place in a stand mixer with a dough hook OR on a floured surface and flour your hands; knead for approximately 5-8 minutes to form a strong, pliable dough. Use the same method as the bread, adding all ingredients together and then kneading on a floured surface until smooth.

Allow to prove in a greased bowl and cover with a clean, wet cloth for about 25 – 45 minutes in a warm spot.

Roll out and then cut into doughnuts and 'holes'.

Allow to prove for a further 15 – 20 minutes and then fry in a medium heat oil.

Dust in cinnamon sugar or with vanilla glaze.

You can also do chocolate drizzles or pipe these full of jam or custard.

Seeded Wholemeal Wraps

SERVINGS: 6-8

INGREDIENTS

450g bakers flour or use half and half white and wholemeal
2 teaspoons dried yeast
1 teaspoon sugar and 1 teaspoon extra flour
320ml lukewarm water (or half water/half milk)
10g salt
30ml olive oil
Half a cup of assorted seeds

METHOD

Add the yeast to the warm water/milk and sugar, 1 teaspoon extra flour, stir and set aside until the yeast has started to bubble and foam.

Place the flour, selected seeds or ingredients such as olives, nigella seeds, edible petals, porcini, etc in a large bowl and add the yeasty water mixture and oil. Mix until it forms a firm dough. Place on a floured bench or in a machine with the dough hook and knead for 5-7 minutes.

Place the dough into a greased bowl cover with a clean wet cloth, and allow to prove until doubled in size (at least 15 minutes on a warm day, longer if it's cool). Remove from the bowl and divide into 8 -12 equal parts, depending on the size needed.

Roll out dinner plate size and then cook in a dry pan for a few minutes on each side or until nicely browned.

Serve with the smoked chicken and salad as a wrap or as dipping bread!
Top with ideas like scented olive oils, sexy cheeses, shaved prosciutto or the toppings of your choice.

Bespoke Culinary Bark AKA Water Crackers

SERVINGS: 8-12

INGREDIENTS

1 cup flour
1 teaspoon of chopped herbs
OR 1 teaspoon chopped petals
OR 1 teaspoon seeds
OR 1 teaspoon cracked black pepper
OR 1 teaspoon dried mushroom powder
OR mix and match these to match your dip cheese or pate.
80 ml water + 20ml melted butter
OR buttermilk OR olive oil = 100ml total liquid

METHOD

Simply mix the ingredients together to form a soft dough, knead with extra flour until easy to handle. Now roll out teaspoonfuls of dough into long, thin biscuits. Place on an ungreased baking sheet and then bake until just browned in an oven of 200c, about 4-6 minutes or until brown and crisp.
You can watch this on my YOUTUBE channel.

Seed Crackers

SERVINGS: 6-8

INGREDIENTS

1/2 cup sunflower seeds
1/2 cup linseed
1/2 cup flax seeds
1/2 cup chia seeds
1/2 cup pumpkin seeds
2 tablespoons psyllium husk powder
1/2 teaspoon salt
1/2 cup sesame seeds, black or white
1/2 cup warmed and melted coconut oil
1 cup boiling hot water

METHOD

Grease a large baking tray and line it with greased baking paper.
Preheat the oven to about 150C.
Mix all the dry ingredients into a large bowl and then add the hot water and oil. Use a strong spoon to bring the mix together. The chia seeds will activate with the hot water and will help form a gel.

Now press the dough onto the greased baking sheet and press it out into the tray. Pop another piece of parchment paper on top and roll out with your rolling pin to get these nice and thin.
Remove the top piece of paper and then bake for 35-45 minutes, depending on the thickness, until they go crisp and the seeds smell roasted and fragrant.
Ensure you stand by towards the end if you have made these super thin, as the seeds could burn, so remove them when golden brown. Allow to cool and snap apart.

Perfect for cheese boards, snacks, salads, and soups where you need a sexy crunch.
Keep in an airtight container in the fridge or freezer to help extend the shelf life.

Pastries

"Life is short and unpredictable. Eat the dessert first." - Helen Keller

Puff Pastry (Pâte Feuilletée)

SERVINGS: 6-8

INGREDIENTS

225 g plain flour
150ml iced water
30g butter, grated
Pinch of salt
100g butter cut into thick slices

METHOD

Place a tile in the freezer to cool if it's a hot day and you need a cool surface!

Mix the flour and the 30g butter together until the butter has been worked through the flour and there are no lumps. Add the salt to the water to dissolve, and then add the water all in one go.
Bring it together with a strong spoon and then use your hands to form a dough ball, putting a little flour on your hands so it doesn't stick.
Knead for about 30 seconds to a minute until a smooth dough ball is formed.
Set aside and cool in the fridge for 10 minutes while you form the butter pat.

While the dough is resting in the fridge, take the 100g butter slices and form into a rectangle of approximately 160 x 120 mm.
Now roll out the dough to an A4 size and place the butter rectangle on one-third of the dough.
Fold it in thirds, making sure all the edges are sealed, and the butter is well hidden.

Roll out to just bigger than an A4 size again, fold into thirds again, turn 90 degrees, roll and fold at least two more times, sometimes three is best; the butter should be well distributed into layers.

Chill for 20 minutes, and then roll out to about 3-5mm and use as desired or freeze for next time.

Rough Puff Pastry

SERVINGS: 6-8

INGREDIENTS

225g plain flour
Pinch of salt
150g butter, cold but not hard
150ml iced cold water

METHOD

Sift the flour and salt into a large bowl.
Cut the butter into 1cm cubes and toss in the flour. Please don't cut the cubes any bigger or else they will pierce the dough and cause problems.
Stir in the water quickly with a spoon to form a soft, pliable dough.

Roll out lightly and evenly, making sure you keep the pastry cool to a 10 x 30 cm rectangle.
Mark into three sections and then fold one end over the middle and the opposite end over that to make an open ended parcel.

Seal the edges with your hand or rolling pin.
Turn so that the fold is on the right, and then roll and fold in the same way for three more turns. This will create lovely layers in the pastry.

Use to make palmiers, vol au vent or sausage rolls and more.

Pâte Brisée (French Shortcrust)

SERVINGS: 6-8

INGREDIENTS

225 g plain flour
25 g caster sugar (for sweet recipes only)
50g cold butter, grated
50 g lard or white fat (or use more butter)
Pinch of salt
1 whole egg
1 tablespoon iced water
2 drops vanilla extract

METHOD

Place a tile in the freezer to cool if it's a hot day and you need a cool surface.
You can also do this in your stand mixer with the batter paddle if you prefer; you would just mix to combine and then rest the dough. Or...
Sift the flour and the salt onto a cool surface and make a well in the centre. Add the sugar, grated butter, egg, water and vanilla. Using your fingertips one hand only, pinch and peck at the ingredients to bring it all together, taking care not to overhandle as the pastry will toughen; always underhandle and always keep cool. Add a few drops of water if it is too dry. Bring the pastry into a ball and then rest in the fridge for 30 minutes in plastic wrap before rolling it out.
This pastry is delicate; roll it out on a floured surface, and always flour your rolling pin, too. A great stress reliever is to place the pastry ball in between two pieces of plastic wrap or two plastic pastry boards and roll it out to about 3-5mm. You can then 'peel' back one of the boards or sheets of plastic and transport the dough into the pastry tin.

NOTE:
This pastry must be rolled thinly to give it the crispness it is famous for.
Never add too much flour when handling and rolling; it will toughen up. Use only cold water.
Always use plain flour, NOT bakers flour; we want low-protein flour.

Shortest Short Crust (Pâte Sucrée)

SERVINGS: 6-8

INGREDIENTS

100 g plain flour
50 g caster sugar
50g cold butter, grated
Pinch of salt
2 egg yolks
2 drops vanilla extract

METHOD

Place a tile in the freezer to cool if it's a hot day and you need a cool surface.

You can also do this in your stand mixer with the batter paddle if you prefer; you would just mix to combine and then rest the dough. Or...

Sift the flour and the salt onto a cool surface and make a well in the centre. Add the sugar, grated butter, egg yolks and vanilla.

Using your fingertips one hand only, pinch and peck at the ingredients to bring it all together, taking care not to overhandle as the pastry will toughen; always underhandle and always keep cool. Bring the pastry into a ball and then rest in the fridge for 30 minutes in plastic wrap before rolling it out.

This pastry is delicate; roll it out on a floured surface, and always flour your rolling pin, too. A great stress reliever is to place the pastry ball in between two pieces of plastic wrap or two plastic pastry boards and roll it out to about 3-5mm. You can then 'peel' back one of the boards or sheets of plastic and transport the dough into the pastry tin.

NOTE:

This pastry must be rolled thinly to give it the crispness it is famous for.
Never add too much flour when handling and rolling; it will toughen up.
Always use plain flour, NOT bakers flour; we want low-protein flour.
No liquid is required because of the high-fat content.

Phyllo Pastry

SERVINGS: 6-8

INGREDIENTS

2 cups plain flour
¾ cup warm water
½ teaspoon salt
60 ml vegetable oil
a mixture of cornflour and flour to dust the work surface, about a quarter cup of each

METHOD

Simply mix the flour, warm water, salt and oil together in a bowl. Mix together to form a ball of dough using a good, strong spoon. Now, place onto a floured surface and knead until smooth and pliable.

Place in some cling film and allow to rest in the fridge for about 15 minutes. Divide into 4 or five pieces, shape each piece into a ball and then roll out, using a flour surface and flour rolling pin and making sure you keep the dough from sticking to the surface by moving it or turning it over often. This is NO fun at all if you just roll and roll because it will stick and stick! Remember, flour is your friend when handling dough.
To get the dough really thin, use your hands and work from the middle to the outside to stretch the dough super thin.

Use immediately or roll into a sausage using cling wrap as a layer between the sheets so they don't stick. Brilliant to use in baklava, toppings as pies, and so many other decadent desserts!
It can be stored and used later.

Choux Pastry

SERVINGS: 8-12

INGREDIENTS

80g Butter

100ml water

100ml milk

Sieve 125g plain flour.

Pinch of salt

2 teaspoons sugar

3 eggs

(the size of the egg will vary; if your paste is TOO dry,
simply add a teaspoon of water to adjust, rather have it too dry than too wet)

METHOD

Heat oven 180C-200C, if possible cook in combination over with a shot of steam.

Place a dish of water in the oven if no combination oven is available.

Melt butter in water, add sieved flour & salt and stir with wooden spoon until mixture leaves the side of the pan. Stir to cook out the flour.

Leave the mixture to cool.

When the mixture is cool, add one egg at a time. The mixture must be of a dropping consistency.

Pipe paste into round puffs, éclairs or Paris breast shapes.

TIPS

- Do not open the oven after you put your choux in –you will flatten your pastry.
- When you add the tray, throw a little water on the bottom of the oven to give a surge of steam to help with the puff of your pastry.
- Can shape when piping into a round, éclairs-doughnut –for Paris Breast shapes.
- Fill with cream | crème patissiere | or a mix of both = Eugene.
- Glace with one of these options spun sugar, choc, fondant, icing sugar and water mix.

Choux Au Craqelin

SERVINGS: MAKES ABOUT 35 MINI CREAM PUFFS

INGREDIENTS

CRAQUELIN
- 60g butter, room temperature
- 70g light brown sugar
- 70g flour
- 1 tablespoon cocoa powder

CHANTILLY CREAM
- 600ml cream
- 60g castor sugar
- 1 teaspoon vanilla extract

CHOUX PASTRY
- 125g plain flour
- 100ml milk
- 100ml water
- 10g sugar
- 2g salt
- 80g unsalted butter
- 3 eggs (the size of the egg will vary. If your paste is TOO dry, simply add a teaspoon of water to adjust; rather have it too dry than too wet)

METHOD

Prepare the craquelin. In a bowl, cream together the butter and sugar, using a spatula or wooden spoon. Add flour and mix until combined. Divide the mixture in two and add cocoa powder in one half of it. Put the dough between two sheets of plastic wrap or parchment paper and roll the dough until very thin, about 2-3 mm thick. Refrigerate the two pieces of dough for 1-2 hours or freeze for 30-45 mins.

Meanwhile, prepare the choux pastry. Sift the flour. In a saucepan, bring the milk, water, sugar, salt and butter to a boil. Remove from heat, add flour all at once, and incorporate, mixing energetically with a wooden spoon until homogenous. Return the saucepan over low heat, and while stirring, cook for 1 minute or two to pull out the moisture from the batter and until it pulls away from the sides of the pan. You will see some of the dough sticks to the bottom of the pan. Transfer batter to a large bowl and allow to cool. Add the eggs one at a time, carefully incorporating each into the batter using a wooden spoon or even a stand mixer. It will result in a smooth, homogenous batter that still holds its shape. Preheat oven to 350F (180C).

Fit a pastry bag with a large ½ inch (1cm) round tip and pipe the dough into 1-inch (3 cm) circles on a parchment paper-lined baking sheet. Remove the craquelin dough from the freezer or fridge and cut 1-inch (3cm) discs using a cookie cutter or a piping tip. Place the discs on top of the choux, pressing slightly. Bake for 25-30 minutes until browned and puffed.

Prick each with a skewer to release steam and allow to cool on a wire rack.

Prepare Chantilly Cream. In a large bowl, whip the cream with an electric mixer until it forms stiff peaks. Add sugar and vanilla extract and mix to combine.

Use a piping bag with a small plain tip to pipe the cream inside the choux from the bottom of it. Refrigerate until ready to serve.

Cream Cheese Pastry

SERVINGS: 4-8

INGREDIENTS

125g butter
200g flour
Pinch salt
125g cream cheese or crème fraîche

BLING: Add matching bling to really show your guests you are really cheffy and creative.
Add 1 teaspoon black pepper and 1 teaspoon lemon zest to really get a round of applause for this; you can really mix and match it depending on your filling!

METHOD

THIS IS MY GO-TO PASTRY. I love it and use it for so many different dishes.

Grate the butter into the flour and then pinch in till the flour resembles breadcrumbs and the butter is evenly distributed. Add the salt, bling, and cream cheese and mix through or use a food processor to combine. Do not overwork the dough! Roll into a dough ball, then cover and chill for about an hour before rolling out and using as desired! Perfect for sweet or savoury dishes.

Tempura Batter

SERVINGS: 4-6

INGREDIENTS

½ cup cornflour
½ cup plain flour
1.5 cup soda or water ICE COLD
1 egg beaten
pinch of salt to season

METHOD

The trick to an excellent crunchy batter is using freezing-cold liquid. Place ingredients in a bowl and mix to make a thin, runny batter. Dust the item to be coated in a bit of flour, then into the batter and straight into some waiting hot vegetable oil. Cook till golden, and then drain and serve.

Yorkshire Puddings

Basic Batter

SERVINGS: 4-8

INGREDIENTS

100g plain flour
1 large egg
300ml milk
30 ml water
pinch of salt
2 tablespoon oil or melted butter

METHOD

This batter can be used to make Yorkshire Puddings, fritters, pancakes and more. Simply sift the flour into a bowl. Make a well in the centre and start by adding the egg and a third of the milk, and mix the batter to incorporate the liquid into the flour. Gradually beat in the rest of the ingredients, and then refrigerate or set aside for at least 20 minutes before use.

Yorkshire Puddings

SERVINGS: 4-6

INGREDIENTS

1 batch of the basic batter recipe above
50-80 ml vegetable oil

METHOD

Pour approximately 80 ml oil into a roasting tray or individual muffin tins. Pop the oiled tray into a preheated oven of 200 C until the oil is SMOKING hot. Please be careful handling this. Now, use a ladle to spoon the batter onto the baking tray or muffin tray in spoonfuls, and then pop it back into the oven for approximately 12-20 minutes until the batter has risen and is golden. The cooking time will depend on the size of the batter, so accordingly. You can then serve these as part of a delicious meal.

Basic Scones

SERVINGS: 6-8

INGREDIENTS

2 cups cake flour sifted

2 teaspoons baking powder sifted

2 pinches salt

2 eggs beaten and placed in a 250ml cup measure

top to the 250 ml mark with milk, sour milk, or even plain yogurt

125ml butter, melted or very very soft

METHOD

Mix all the ingredients together until a nice thick batter is formed; try not to over-mix, as these will become tough if overhandled. Less is more in this case.

Drop tablespoons of the mixture into greased and floured muffin tins, paper cups, terracotta pots, or just dollop onto a baking sheet. Bake at 180C for about 15 minutes until golden brown and cooked. Check for doneness. Serve with delicious butter.

Sweet Options for Scones

Add 2 tablespoons white sugar to the dry ingredients,
as well as a teaspoon vanilla or almond essence to make them sweet scones.

CHOCOLATE SCONES

Grate in 100g milk chocolate to make delicious chocolate muffins or chop up your favourite chocolate bar

BLUEBERRY SCONES

Add 2 tablespoons strawberry, blueberry or fig jam to the mix for fruity muffins,
serve with dollops of vanilla and whipped cream

LEMON & POPPY SCONES

Add the zest of one lemon or lime and a tablespoon of poppy seeds

Savoury Options for Scones

Simply add this to basic recipe, no need to adjust quantities.

FETA, PIQUANT PEPPER & CHIVE SCONES

Crumble 100g Feta. 2 tablespoons chopped piquant peppers and 2 tablespoons chopped chives into the mixture. You can use parsley, sage or similar instead (nice for colour)

WASABI & SALMON SCONES

Add 1 tablespoon wasabi and 100g chopped smoked salmon to the mixture

SUNDRIED TOMATO PESTO SCONES

Just add 2 teaspoons or a little more tomato pesto to your mixture

BASIL PESTO SCONES

As above, just add 2 teaspoons basil pesto

MUSTARD & SAGE SCONES

Add 2 teaspoons grainy mustard and 1 teaspoon chopped sage to the mix

Other Varieties to Mix & Match

CHOPPED OLIVES, CHOPPED SUN-DRIED TOMATOES
ONION, SESAME OR POPPY SEEDS
GRATED ONION AND GARLIC
CHEDDAR, BLUE, PARMESAN OR PECORINO CHEESE
HAM, COOKED BACON, COOKED MUSHROOMS

Spiced Caramel Fig Rusks with Pistachio for Sexy Cheeseboards

SERVINGS: 8-12

INGREDIENTS

1 cup whole-wheat flour
1 cup plain flour
1 teaspoon baking powder
1/2 teaspoon bicarbonate of soda
1/2 teaspoon salt
2 cups buttermilk
1/4 cup raw or dark sugar 1/4 cup honey OR malt

NOW YOU CAN HAVE FUN MIXING AND MATCHING. Often, it depends on the cheese or dip you are serving this with. So have fun, and think ahead.
Seeds: add FOUR of the following.

1/2 cup flax seed, ground
1/2 cup roasted pumpkin seeds
1/2 cup pecans, chopped
1/2 cup sesame seeds
1/2 cup apricots
1/2 cup dried figs, chopped
1/2 cup chopped hazelnuts
1 tablespoon chopped fresh rosemary
1/2 cup raisins or dried cranberries
1/2 cup figs
Zest of one orange
Pinch of spice of your choice: try cinnamon/nutmeg/ras el hanout

METHOD

Simply mix all of your ingredients together to form a batter and then bake in a loaf tin for approximately 19-25 minutes until cooked through.
Cool, and then slice very thinly! These will be easier to slice once they are cool!
Then place on a baking tray and dry out for about 1 hour at 80c until nice and crisp!

You'll have so much making these! You can easily match any cheese or dip you want!

Pasta, Pizza & Gnocchi

Basic Pasta Recipe

SERVINGS: 3-4

INGREDIENTS

300g '00' flour
3 large eggs
10ml water depending on the size of an egg; you will need less if you use an XL or Jumbo egg

METHOD

Simply combine all the ingredients together in a large bowl using a strong spoon. Once you have incorporated all of the moist ingredients into the flour, place the dough onto a floured surface, dust your hands with flour, and then knead, adding flour the minute the dough sticks to your hands. It should eventually go nice and smooth and elastic and pliable. Place in a lightly greased bowl under a wet cloth or in plastic wrap, and rest for about 20 minutes in the fridge or on the bench.

Please watch my videos on my YOUTUBE channel for a full demo.

It is now ready to either hand roll OR put through a pasta machine.

To get the dough ready to roll out nice and thin, divide the dough in half using a strong knife. Roll each piece into a rough rectangle, about 'earlobe' thick. It should then be able to go through your pasta roller on the widest setting.

Always dust with flour to prevent the dough from sticking back to itself. Continue until you reach the desired thickness, and then use a knife or the pasta machine to cut into the pasta shape you require.

You can use it straight away or allow it to dry.

Roasted Pumpkin & Speck Ravioli with Burnt Sage Butter

SERVINGS: 4-6

INGREDIENTS

PASTA
300g 'OO' soft fine flour
3 large free-range eggs
10ml water

EGG WASH
1 egg whisked with 60ml water

BURNT SAGE BUTTER SAUCE
100g salted butter
12-24 fresh sage leaves

FILLING
2 cups roasted pumpkin, slightly mashed
1/2 cup fresh ricotta/or use parmesan grated (to taste)
½ cup finely diced and cooked speck/bacon bits
1 teaspoon freshly chopped garlic
Salt and pepper to season
1 teaspoon fresh oregano, basil and thyme

GARNISH
Freshly grated Parmesan or Pecorino

METHOD

PASTA

Place the flour, eggs and water in a bowl and mix with a large, strong spoon, stirring to bring everything together to form a rough ball. When you can form a rough ball, place it on a floured work surface and knead the dough until smooth. Place to rest in a greased bowl and cover with a clean, wet cloth for at least 20 minutes before rolling as required.

FILLING

Simply mix together and use them to stuff the ravioli.

Also, don't forget to use egg wash or else your ravioli will unravel.

And always cook in lots of boiling salted water.

When the ravioli rise to the surface, they are done, about 6-8 minutes (if they are full of air bubbles, they will rise sooner, so always test one to make sure)

BURNT SAGE BUTTER SAUCE

Simply brown 100g butter over a low heat with fresh sage leaves, and use this gorgeous fragranced butter to drizzle and lift the flavour of the ravioli.

Add lemon/lime zest for a flavour sensation. You can also use sugo or the roasted capsicum puree here.

HOW TO ASSEMBLE

Start by cutting the dough into two pieces.

Store the other piece under plastic wrap until you use it; do not let it go dry.

Start rolling your rested pasta dough ball into a messy rectangle about the size of your phone, and roll until about as thick as your earlobe. Dust with flour and pass through a pasta roller on the widest setting OR you can also roll into a long, thin rectangle simply by using a rolling pin.

If you are using a pasta machine, keep dropping down to a thinner press on each roll. Keep dusting with flour to make sure it doesn't stick and become stressful and annoying!

You have the perfect pasta when you throw some flour down on the bench, draw a letter or a love heart into the flour, place the rolled dough on top, and if it's thin enough, you should be able to 'see' or 'read' the make you made through the dough.

I use a ravioli tray, but you can also use a ravioli press or cutter.

Lay one layer of the thin pasta down and brush with egg wash. Fill with a spoonful of filling, leaving a neat edge for the border. When you have made a row of spoons of filling, top it with another layer of thin dough. Press to seal, and then use your ravioli press, ravioli cutter or just a sharp paring knife to make perfect little stuffed pillows. Place on a tray in a single layer on until all is completed, and then boil for 6-8 minutes in lots of boiling salted water. If they rise to the surface, they have an air bubble and are not done.

Drain, toss in some fresh olive oil, and then add the sauce of your choice and lots of grated Pecorino.

Ravishing Roasted Spinach & Ricotta Ravioli with Burnt Sage & Pine Nut Butter

SERVINGS: 4-6

INGREDIENTS

PASTA
300g "OO' soft fine flour
3 large free-range eggs
10ml water

EGG WASH
1 egg whisked with 30ml water

FILLING
150g baby or chopped spinach
300g fresh ricotta
60-70g Parmesan cheese finely grated
1 teaspoon freshly chopped garlic
Salt and pepper to season
1 teaspoon fresh oregano or sage

METHOD

PASTA
Place the flour, eggs, and water in a bowl and mix with a large strong spoon, stirring to bring everything together to form a rough ball. When you can form a rough ball, place it on a floured work surface and knead the dough until smooth. Place to rest in a greased bowl and cover with a clean, wet cloth for at least 20 minutes before rolling as required.

FILLING
Simply mix together and use the wonderful filling to stuff the ravioli as per the previous recipe instructions… don't forget to use egg wash, or else your ravioli will unravel, and always cook in lots of boiling salted water. Cook the ravioli for about 6-8 minutes (if they are full of air bubbles, they will rise sooner, so always test one to make sure)

BURNT SAGE AND PINE NUT BUTTER
Simply brown 100g butter over low heat with about 12 fresh sage leaves and 2 tablespoons pine nuts and use this gorgeous fragranced butter to drizzle and lift the flavour of the ravioli. Add lemon zest for a flavour sensation.

TO SERVE
Serve the gorgeous ravioli with the roasted capsicum sauce and the burnt butter sauce, and live happily ever after!

Change your Life Bolognaise

Change your Life Bolognaise

SERVINGS: 4-6

INGREDIENTS

1kg premium beef mince
1 large onion finely sliced
3-6 cloves garlic
3 tablespoons fresh oregano/thyme/marjoram or use 1 teaspoon dried Italian herb mix
1 carrot finely diced or grated
1 celery stalk finely grated
1 pinch nutmeg (very important!)
80ml milk
3 tablespoons olive oil
2-3 teaspoons beef stock powder or 2 stock cubes
1 tin chopped tomatoes
1 jar passata (500-700ml)

METHOD

The first thing you should do is heat and grease a large pan until it is just about smoking hot. Now add the mince…we want the mince to sizzle when it hits the pan, and IT SHOULD SIZZLE nice and loud and sexy.

DO NOT STIR. I know you are worried about this burning, and you are also worried about lumps, but let the mince brown and seal on the first side you put down FIRST and let the pan heat up again, and THEN you can stir ever so slightly just to get some more mince onto the base of the pan. My favourite mince 'fluffer' is one of those cheap plastic-coated whisks you get at the supermarket that only have about 4 loops. If you don't have one of those, use a strong plastic spoon or egg flip to break down the mince.

Once the mince is brown and fragrant and sexy ALL BY ITSELF, then and only then do you add the finely chopped onion and garlic. There should be enough oil out of the mince that you have rendered off during your amazing sizzle-cooking of the mince at a nice high heat. If not, add the olive oil. You can stir as much as you like now by the way, that mince is SEALED off! Now add the herbs, nutmeg, milk, stock powder, grated/diced carrot, and seasoning and stir through. Amazing colour, isn't it?

Finally, add the chopped tomatoes, vegetables, and passata, and you're practically done. Turn down the heat and let that all cook through, and then check the seasoning, and it's ready to serve. This way of cooking will not only save you time, BUT it will add valuable flavour and vibrant personality to your otherwise boring mince.
Serve with fresh al dente spaghetti, shaved parmesan, and lots of freshly chopped parsley.

Authentic Pizza

Authentic Pizza Base

SERVINGS: 6-8

INGREDIENTS

DOUGH	**PIZZA SAUCE**
1kg "OO" or bakers flour	3 tablespoons olive oil to fry
650ml cold water	1 brown onion, finely chopped
15g salt	2 cloves garlic
2g instant yeast	1 tablespoon freshly chopped marjoram or oregano
	(or use 1 teaspoon dried)
TO HANDLE DOUGH AND ROLL	500ml tomato passata
Semolina, about 1 cup	salt and pepper to season
	1 fresh chilli optional

METHOD

This is the best-ever pizza base recipe, BUT it does rely on a 24-hour proving time. It is easy and reliable and gives a very authentic result. If you are doing this in your oven at home, I recommend a pizza stone and I also recommend pre-heating it at at least 280 C for 20-30 minutes. Remember, in the pizza ovens in restaurants they get their base heat of the stone to upwards of 320 C...so hot is essential for an authentic puff and browning of the base for a good flavour and crunch.

Fry the onions and the garlic in the oil until just soft. Now add the tomato passata/puree, herbs and the seasoning and cook through. Adjust seasonings. Allow to cool and then store in the fridge. Best pizza sauce but also a fantastic sauce for all sorts of pasta and mains.

To make the dough, add all these ingredients together, except for the semolina, and knead for 5-8 minutes with a stand mixer and dough hook. Divide into four or six dough balls and cover with a wet cloth or wrap, and then store in the fridge for at least 12 hours or overnight.

Hand stretch the dough ball using your semolina on the bench. the easiest way to do this is to start by pressing the dough thinner from the middle to the outside, leaving a lovely thick edge. Turn the dough and keep working from the middle to the outside. Now top with sauce using a metal spoon; you can thin your dough a little using the back of the spoon, but KEEP THAT BORDER nice and thick. Top with your favourite ingredients, and then bake hot and fast, turning as you go, until you have a brown and crunchy base. A pizza oven base should be really hot, so ensure you have pre-heated it for at least half an hour.

There are three official variants of Neapolitan pizza:
PIZZA MARINARA: Topped with tomato, garlic, oregano, and extra-virgin olive oil.
PIZZA MARGHERITA: Topped with tomato, fresh sliced mozzarella, fresh basil, and extra-virgin olive oil.
PIZZA MARGHERITA EXTRA: Topped with tomato, sliced mozzarella di Bufala/fior di latte, fresh basil, and extra-virgin olive oil.

Rustic Italian Gnocchi

Rustic Italian Gnocchi with Burnt Sage Butter & Pancetta Bark

SERVINGS: 4

INGREDIENTS

GNOCCHI

500g dry, cooked potato mash
150g potato starch/plain flour
Pinch of salt

SAUCE AND GARNISH

80g salted butter
12-18 sage leaves whole and fresh
80g Pancetta finely sliced and roasted until crispy

METHOD

CHEF'S NOTE:
I recommend buying a potato ricer if you plan on making lots of gnocchi; it makes this job so much easier.

Brush and wash the potatoes and then boil until tender in salted water. Drain and then mash while hot.

Add the flour and the salt, and then mix to form a firm dough.
Place on a floured surface and knead for about a minute to form a soft, pliable dough.
Flour a work surface and then roll about a handful of gnocchi dough into a long cylinder.

Cut with a palette or butter knife into tiny 'balls'. Shape it with a gnocchi paddle/fork if required, or simply leave it in a rustic shape. Boil in salted water until they rise to the surface, about 3-5 minutes. Drain.

In a pan, heat the butter and the sage and add the gnocchi. When the butter starts to bubble and the white foam has turned to golden and is smelling nutty and fragrant you can remove it from the heat and serve. Serve with fresh micro herbs, pancetta, and grated pecorino cheese.

OPTIONAL
Griddled tomatoes or mushrooms

Parmesan Gnocchi Roman Style

SERVINGS: 4-6

INGREDIENTS

3 cups milk
150g butter
300g semolina fine
2 eggs beaten
100g parmesan
Salt and pepper to taste

METHOD

Bring the milk and, butter, and seasoning to a boil, making sure you stir well so as not to burn the milk. Remove from heat and whisk in the semolina; it will go really thick. Put it back on the heat and then boil through. Remove from heat and stir to cool. Now add the beaten eggs and cheese and stir to make a thick paste.

When cool, roll into cylinders and cut into small little dumplings and roll off the back of a fork or gnocchi paddle and then bake with 50g grated cheese and a sauce of your choice until golden and fluffy and brown!

Soups & Salads

Thai Lime, Pea & Coconut Soup with Chilli & Shallot Bling

SERVINGS: 4-6

INGREDIENTS

250g frozen peas

1 tin coconut cream or milk (I prefer coconut cream because it's richer and thicker)

800ml good chicken or vegetable stock

1 tablespoon green curry paste/Chiang Mai paste

1 teaspoon Thai lime DUST (you will need to finely chop some kaffir lime leaves)

1 teaspoon coconut or dark brown sugar

2 tablespoons fish sauce to season

METHOD

Place the peas, coconut milk/cream, stock, curry paste, lime dust and sugar in a saucepan and bring to a boil. Once heated right through you can season to taste with the fish sauce and then blitz to a thin soup with a stick blender. If this is too thick, you can add some more stock or just water, depending on the flavour.

I want a nice, sweet, but well-seasoned result here, with the fish sauce adding that vital saltiness that balances off the sweetness of the peas and the coconut sugar.

Place in a blender, making sure it's not hot when you do so. Blend until smooth and velvety.

Serve into gorgeous plates, making sure you use a transporter plate (aka saucer) when you dish up so you don't drip over the side of the plate. This will make you so much cheffier and tidier.

Now garnish with coconut cream swirl (you will need to have kept some coconut cream aside), chopped chilli, lime dust and Asian shallots.

Almond & Chorizo Gazpacho

SERVINGS: 4-6

INGREDIENTS

200 g fresh shelled almonds or ground almond
1 clove garlic, peeled
50 g sourdough bread, crust removed, soaked in water
1 white onion, diced
300 g sultana grapes, washed and picked
50 ml sherry vinegar or similar sweet vinegar
100 ml extra virgin olive oil, plus extra for serving
Flake salt to season and garnish
Water or stock to thin
1 chorizo sausage, diced finely and cooked hot and fast in a pan. Reserve for garnish.

METHOD

Put the almonds, soaked sourdough, garlic, onion and grapes into a large bowl and use either a bar blender or a hand-held blender to purée all the ingredients together.

Once smooth, leave the blender on the lowest power, add half the vinegar, and slowly drizzle in the oil. Strain to ensure the liquid is smooth.

Taste and adjust seasoning with remaining vinegar, water and salt. Chill and then serve with either bacon, speck or chorizo 'gravel' or simply with seasoned olive oil.

Roast Cauliflower Soup

SERVINGS: 4-6

INGREDIENTS

3 tablespoons butter

1 large onions chopped

1 teaspoon ras el hanout/curry powder turmeric (optional)

1 whole cauliflower

4 cloves garlic peeled

1 litre of vegetable, mushroom or chicken stock

100ml cream

5-10ml truffled olive oil/lemon olive oil/extra virgin olive oil

METHOD

Place the raw, rinsed and cut cauliflower onto a greased roasting tray or in your air fryer. Cut the cauliflower down into smaller pieces so it roasts faster. Place on a tray with the garlic and then drizzle in about 50-80ml olive oil, salt and pepper to season and then roast in swearword hot oven of 220-250 for about 12-15 minutes until brown and delicious.

In a saucepan, cook down 1 finely chopped onion in a little butter over low heat; now add the cauliflower and the garlic and then stir a little. Add 1 Litre vegetable, chicken or mushroom stock and 100ml cream and allow to simmer for 2-3 minutes. Hit this with a stick blender and blend until smooth.
Adjust seasoning, add hot water if it is too thick, check seasoning again and then blend till smooth.

Serve in a sexy bowl, drizzle with a little truffle oil and some micro herb and petal bling.

Thai Green Papaya Salad

Thai Green Papaya Salad

SERVINGS: 4-6

INGREDIENTS

2 cloves of garlic
1-5 bird eyes chillies (fresh or dried)
1 tablespoon roasted peanuts or cashew nut
1 tablespoon fish sauce
½ - 1 tablespoon palm sugar or dark brown sugar
juice of one lime or lemon, about 2-3 tablespoons
3-5 cherry tomatoes
1 cup of shredded green papaya
1 cup long beans or green beans, finely diced or sliced

METHOD

Peel and julienne green papaya using a Thai zig-zag peeler, julienne slicer, or a grater.
Crush the peeled garlic and the chillies (depending on how spicy you prefer) into the mortar. Pound them for a few seconds until the garlic and chillies are crushed. Add green beans and slice cherry tomatoes. Use the pestle to crush green beans and cherry tomatoes until they break up a little bit. Then add ½ tablespoon of palm sugar and 1 tablespoon of fish sauce, and squeeze the juice from the limes into the mortar.
You can always start with less seasoning and add more to your liking.

The last step is to toss in the green papaya shavings.
Mix it all together; make sure the dressing is coating all the green papaya and that the salad is evenly mixed. Top with the roasted nuts before serving.

Thai Grilled Beef Salad

Thai Grilled Beef Salad

SERVINGS: 4-6

INGREDIENTS

1 large steak (sirloin, rib eye)
1 teaspoon freshly ground black pepper
1 teaspoon cooking oil
Pinch of salt
1 tablespoon fish sauce
1 teaspoon palm sugar or dark brown sugar
2 tablespoons lime/lemon juice
1 to 2 tablespoons dried roasted chilli flakes or thinly chopped fresh chilli
1 teaspoon toasted rice powder (dry roast rice in a pan, then crush in blender or mortar and pestle)
1 stalk of lemongrass, sliced diagonally
1-2 small shallots
12 -16 cherry tomatoes
1 small cucumber
2 -3 spring onions, finely chopped
2-3 tablespoons coriander, chopped
2-3 tablespoons fresh mint

METHOD

Leave the beef at room temperature then coat with oil, pepper and salt.
Heat a cast iron pan or large skillet over high heat then cook steak 3 to 4 minutes each side for medium-rare. Don't forget to sear the side of the steak as well.

Remove from heat and let the steak rest for 5 minutes.
Cut the cherry tomatoes in half, thinly slice cucumber, slice shallots, green onions, and coriander thinly and prepare mint by taking leaves off from the stem. Set aside.

Slice steak into ¼-inch thick slices.
In a large mixing bowl, mix fish sauce, palm sugar, lime juice and chilli flakes all together. Taste and adjust by adding more ingredients as you prefer.

Before serving, stir in sliced steak and toss until steak pieces are coated evenly with dressing. Then, put in toasted rice powder and toss in all of the vegetables we prepared easily. Transfer to a serving plate and garnish with toasted rice powder and more chopped chilli if you like.

Kipfler Potato Salad

SERVINGS: 6-8

INGREDIENTS

1 kg Kipfler Potato or use baby potatoes (or just any potato!)
1 small onion finely sliced
100 g bacon or chorizo or speck or prosciutto diced
250g tub sour cream or creme fraiche
3 tablespoons chopped chives or parsley
Salt and pepper to season!

METHOD

Fry the bacon bits in a hot pan until nice and brown and crispy; add the finely chopped onion, reduce the heat and then stir until the onion is soft. Remove pan from heat.

Now add the potatoes that have been cooked and sliced (or leave them whole if they are small) into the bacon and onion mix in the pan and then add the sour cream/creme fraiche, chives, or parsley and then stir to coat.

Season to taste and then serve! I garnished it with edible petals and micro herbs to make this salad look ten times more expensive.

Egg Dishes

How to Poach an Egg
You need to learn how to do this. I promise it's easy!

SERVINGS: 2

INGREDIENTS

Water
Salt to season the water
FRESH eggs kept in the fridge until the very last minute
Vinegar is optional

METHOD

If you have only ever had disaster poaching, it was NOT YOUR FAULT.
It was simply an old egg or warm egg, so forgive yourself and try again.
Keep the eggs in the fridge until the very last minute; the colder the egg, the better your 'luck' will be. I don't like the taste of vinegar, so I don't add it. But you can add 10% vinegar to the water if you can handle the taste.

Grab a frying pan (you can use a saucepan, but a frying pan is easier to retrieve with the slotted spoon later). Grease the base of the frying pan with cooking spray or a little oil, preventing any accidents and sticking later. Fill the frying pan with hot water, enough to cover the height of the eggs. Season the water with about a teaspoon of salt.
Place the pan over medium heat; the water should be at a gentle simmer, not a boil.
Boiling water will agitate your eggs and break them up unnecessarily.
When the water is gently simmering, crack the eggs (as many as you need) carefully into the water. It's best to drop them into the water as low as you can manage.

Get your slotted spoon ready, and keep the water simmering gently.

DO NOT LET THE WATER BOIL!

You might have to adjust as you go. You can see when the eggs are starting to set. For your first few times, you can use the slotted spoon to check how cooked your egg is. If it is ready, take it out using the spoon and then drain it on some paper towel, just to drain the water. Getting rid of the water now will prevent soggy toast.
If the egg is 'wisping' in the water *(spreading out tendrils like a wisp of smoke)*, and if it looks like it may be falling apart, it may just be that the egg is old and that the egg white is old and thin. You can simply 'cut' this wispy egg off with the side of your spoon, and it will look gorgeous again.
Practice makes perfect, and you will get better and better the more you make these.
Remember, you can add 10% vinegar to help 'set' the eggs, but it does dramatically change the flavour, in my opinion.
Happy Poaching.

Eggs Benedict

Eggs Benedict

SERVINGS: 4-6

INGREDIENTS

1 recipe Hollandaise Sauce seasoned with 1 teaspoon Dijon mustard (recipe on page 48)
6 slices ham, heated and cooked
6 English Muffins, toasted and buttered
6 poached eggs
Edible petals, micro herbs or chopped chives/parsley for garnish

METHOD

Grab a frying pan (you can use a saucepan, but a frying pan is easier to retrieve with the slotted spoon later). Grease the base of the frying pan with cooking spray or a little oil; this will prevent any accidents and sticking later. Fill the frying pan with hot water, enough to cover the height of the eggs. Season the water with about a teaspoon of salt.

Place the pan over medium heat; the water should be at a gentle simmer, not a boil.

Boiling water will agitate your eggs and break them up unnecessarily.

When the water is gently simmering, crack the eggs carefully into the water. It's best to drop them into the water as low as you can manage.

Get your slotted spoon ready, and keep the water simmering gently. You might have to adjust as you go. You can see when the eggs are starting to set. For your first few times, you can use the slotted spoon to check how cooked your egg is. If it is ready, take it out using the spoon and then drain it on some paper towel, just to drain the water. Getting rid of the water now will prevent soggy toast.

TO ASSEMBLE:

Place the toasted bread on the plate and top with the cooked ham.
Place the poached egg on top of the ham and then coat the poached egg with the Hollandaise sauce.
Garnish with micro herbs or chopped parsley and petals, and serve.

Easy Omelette

SERVINGS: 2-4

INGREDIENTS

OMELETTE
1 teaspoon butter
2 eggs
1 tablespoon finely chopped herbs of your choice
1 tablespoon water
1 pinch salt
1 pinch pepper

FILLINGS
2-4 tablespoons of the filling of your choice: chopped ham, spinach, bacon, mushrooms, onions, capsicum or cheese

METHOD

To be honest... a great omelette is all about the pan or using enough butter or oil in the pan so it doesn't stick. Go buy a new pan if you have to.

You need a clean, non-stick pan or a stainless steel pan that is totally smooth. My preference is a non-stick.

Grease with a vegetable oil like sunflower or rice bran, but NOT olive oil. Olive oil makes everything stick! Heat the pan gently with the butter. Place the eggs, herbs, seasoning and water into a bowl and beat to form a smooth batter.

When the butter is sizzling gently, pour the entire egg mixture into the pan. Get a plastic egg lift and start gently scraping the egg mix from the edge of the pan to the centre of the pan as it sets. Do this about 4-6 times, and then add the filling.

Now let the egg cook and form a brown crust, ensuring it is not sticking. If it has stuck, spray or grease more next time! Using your egg-lift, tilt the pan, and fold the omelette in half using the egg-lift to help. Slide it onto a plate and serve!

Happy Sexy Quickie Eggs

Happy Sexy Quickie Eggs

SERVINGS: 2

INGREDIENTS

Vegetable oil or cooking spray (not olive oil)
2 tablespoons chopped/diced bacon
OR Prosciutto/Pancetta OR Speck OR chorizo sausage OR mushrooms (you choose)
2 tablespoons chopped onions
OR Spinach OR spring onion OR zucchini OR tomato
3-4 fresh free-range eggs
1 pinch of pepper to season
1 tablespoon grated cheddar
Pecorino or Parmesan (optional)
Drizzle of truffle oil and extra virgin olive oil (optional)

METHOD

In my quest for the laziest YET sexiest eggs, this has become one of my best inventions.
Almost a cross between an omelette and a fried egg - but the best of both!
Omelettes have the privilege of having a filling to make them a bit sexier.
Fried eggs are okay, but the large expanse of tasteless egg white is just not my favourite.
With this recipe, the white will be loaded with amazing flavour, colour and texture and will look ten bucks more expensive. Also, unless you have a fabulous pan, omelettes can make your language very bad when they stick and break and just don't turn out. Literally.
So, try my happy eggs; you can change the 'filling' to whatever you like.
I'll give you a few ideas and let you happy egg all by yourself! Enjoy.

You will need a small to medium frying pan with a lid for this recipe.
Heat and grease the frying pan well with the cooking spray. You DO NOT want to underdo the oiling and risk all your ingredients sticking. Place the diced bacon *(or speck, chorizo or mushrooms)* in the pan and let them go crisp and brown and flavoursome. Now add the second ingredient *(onion, spring onion or zucchini)* and cook while stirring for about a minute until soft.
Now spread it evenly around the pan.
Crack the eggs over this deliciousness and then turn the heat to medium, put the lid on the pan and let those eggs cook through to the doneness you like: soft, medium or hard.
Season with pepper oil, and it's ready to serve!

Starters

A recipe has no soul, you as the cook, must bring soul to the recipe.

Around the world with a Baked Brie Fondue

Around the world with a Baked Brie Fondue

METHOD

This is a gorgeous and glamorous take on the everyday cheeseboard. Baking Brie or even a delicious Camembert will transform it into the most delicious baked oozy cheesy treat, and the best part is that it's super simple.

We can also transform this fantastic fondue into many global flavours just by adding a few glorious ingredients to change the theme. Try these or try your own idea; you'll be doing this dish for many years to come. You'll have travelled the world in no time!

For all the recipes below, start with the Brie or Camembert and place it on a plate that is ovenproof; I use a soup bowl or similar (most of them are ovenproof!)

FRENCH INFLUENCE

Make a paste with 1 clove of minced garlic and 1 teaspoon of chopped tarragon/rosemary/thyme, and then rub over the cheese to coat it in this fragrant paste. Bake for 8-12 minutes in a hot oven of 200c until it has puffed up and the cheese is oozy and melting. Garnish with freshly chopped edible petals like roses, borage, pansies, dianthus or carnations.

MIDDLE EASTERN INFLUENCE

Place a tablespoon of creamed or plain honey on the cheese and bake for 8-12 minutes in a hot oven of 200c until it has puffed up the cheese is oozy and melting, and the honey is caramelised and melted. Now add a teaspoon of chopped nuts (pistachio or hazelnut) and a light dusting of cumin powder or ras el hanout spice and serve garnished with the petals I've mentioned above.

AFRICAN INFLUENCE

Bake for 8-12 minutes in a hot oven of 200c until it has puffed up and the cheese is oozy and melting. Garnish with freshly chopped chilli, biltong/jerky chopped up really fine and a little bit of lemon or lime zest and chopped chilli...garnish with petals and serve!

SPANISH INFLUENCE

Chop about 80g chorizo sausage up until it looks like mince, fry quickly in a hot pan until just browning, add 2 tablespoons finely sliced onion and a large sprinkle of paprika. Add a teaspoon of lemon zest and then place this on the cheese and bake for 8-12 minutes in a hot oven of 200c until it has puffed up and the cheese is oozy and melting. Garnish with strips of fire-roasted capsicum diced finely and a sprinkle of freshly chopped parsley.

STICKY ASIAN

Mix 1 tablespoon of plum jam to a paste with half a teaspoon of fresh ginger and place on top of the cheese. Bake for 8-12 minutes in a hot oven of 200c until it has puffed up and the cheese is oozy and melting.

Fragrant Spring Garlic & Tarragon Brie

SERVINGS: 2

INGREDIENTS

1 x Brie or Camembert
2 cloves garlic, finely sliced
12 tarragon sprigs, thyme, sage or rosemary

METHOD

Simply stud with the garlic and the herbs, bake in a hot oven for 8 minutes, and serve!
Or, simply bake the cheese and then drizzle with honey and dukkah!

Butternut & Feta Hummus

SERVINGS: 4-6

INGREDIENTS

1 tin chickpeas in brine, drained
1 large clove garlic, crushed
1 teaspoon ground cumin (jeera)
2 tablespoons cooked mashed pumpkin or sweet potato
2 tablespoons crumbled feta
Juice and zest of a lime
2 teaspoons tahini paste or just use 2 tablespoons plain yogurt
Salt and pepper to season

GARNISH

Extra virgin olive oil, pine nuts, fresh coriander, chickpeas, mint leaves

METHOD

Keep a handful of chickpeas as a garnish. Blend all the ingredients except for the garnish together in a blender and blend until smooth.

Place in a large flat bowl and garnish with the toasted seeds, coriander and a drizzle of the oil.

Tarragon Scented Paté with Shiraz & Strawberry Jelly

Tarragon Scented Paté with Shiraz & Strawberry Jelly

SERVINGS: 6

INGREDIENTS

TARRAGON PATÉ
- 80g salted butter
- 500 g chicken livers OR sliced mushrooms
- 1 medium onion sliced
- 1 teaspoon fresh tarragon or thyme chopped
- 2 cloves garlic crushed
- 100 g cold smoked bacon chopped
- 50 ml chicken stock
- 50 ml brandy (optional)
- 60 ml Cream

SHIRAZ & STRAWBERRY JELLY
- 125ml shiraz wine
- 80 ml strawberry puree or cordial
- 50ml white or dark balsamic vinegar
- 2 sheets gelatine, soaked in cold water for 30-60 seconds until soft, then squeeze to remove water and add to hot liquid

METHOD

Trim the chicken livers if necessary, rinse and pat dry.

Melt the butter in a frying pan, and then when hot, fry the bacon until brown and crisp.

Add the onions, herbs and the garlic and allow to cook through.

Now fambé with the brandy using matches or your gas cooktop to ignite the brandy.

Shake and allow the alcohol to burn off.

Add livers OR the mushrooms, and cook livers till slightly pink inside; do not overcook them as they will be grainy. Add the thyme and liquids, leaving the cream for last.

Season to taste and then allow to cool once chicken livers have cooked through.

Place in blender and blend until smooth.

Place in ramekin dishes or other suitable dish and top with jelly OR you can top with extra virgin olive oil or burnt or melted butter if you prefer.

SHIRAZ AND STRAWBERRY JELLY

Heat all the ingredients and allow to reduce by half in a pan.

Remove the pan from heat and then add the bloomed gelatine.

Stir until the gelatine has dissolved.

Pour over the top of the smoothed pate and then chill until set!

Serve with Melba toast or fresh bread - delicious!

Tarragon Scented Paté served with Crostini

SERVINGS: 6

INGREDIENTS

100 g cold smoked bacon/speck chopped
500 g chicken livers OR mushrooms
1 medium onion sliced
2 cloves garlic crushed
100 ml chicken stock
50 ml brandy (optional)
1 teaspoon fresh thyme
60 ml cream

METHOD

Trim the chicken livers if necessary, rinse, and pat dry. Heat the frying pan, and then when the swear word is hot, fry the bacon until brown and crisp. Add the onions and the garlic and allow to cook through.

Now add livers OR the mushrooms, cook livers till slightly pink inside, do not overcook them as they will be grainy. Add the tarragon and stock. Allow to cook through and almost dry out, then scrape the food to the side of the pan so that it is 'clean' and will heat up.

Once hot, add the brandy, and when bubbling, ignite. TAKE CARE, but the flame will only go upwards, so please avert your face! Shake while flaming to release the alcohol, and then the flames will die out. Add the cream to last. Season to taste and then allow to cool.

Place in blender and blend until smooth. Place in ramekin dishes or other suitable dishes and top with extra virgin olive oil or melted butter if you are not serving the patè straight away.

Serve with melba toast, crostini or fresh bread….delicious!

Duck & Pork Terrine with Cranberries & Pistachios

SERVINGS: 8-12

INGREDIENTS

2 duck (or chicken breasts), about 300g skin on for roasting
400g thinly sliced streaky bacon rashers or prosciutto to wrap your terrine
800g pork shoulder, cubed
1 cup breadcrumbs soaked in 50ml milk
3 shallots or one medium onion, roughly chopped
1 large garlic clove, roughly chopped
200g duck or chicken livers, roughly chopped
1 teaspoon crushed black peppercorns

2 pinches nutmeg
1 teaspoon salt
pinch cinnamon, ground
50ml brandy or cognac or whisky
2 eggs, beaten
50g shelled pistachio kernels
50g sultanas, cranberries, raisins *or dried apricots diced*

METHOD

Heat oven to 180C. Put the duck or chicken breasts with their skin on, season lightly with salt and then place in a shallow dish. Roast in the hot oven for 20 mins or until brown and cooked. Reserve the fat, but discard the skin. then, pour the duck fat into a bowl to cool. Reserve 10 bacon rashers to line your terrine dish, and then roughly chop the remainder.

Roughly chop the cooked duck meat. The secret to a delicious terrine is the fat content. But this will render off during cooking.

In a food processor, blend the chopped bacon, pork and duck in batches to a coarse texture, then place into a large bowl. Soak in the milk for 5 mins. Squeeze out the bread and put it in the food processor with the shallots, garlic and livers. Process to a coarse texture, then add to the bowl, mixing well.

Add the spices to the meat along with about four tablespoons of the reserved duck fat, Cognac, eggs, pepper and salt. Mix together very thoroughly with your hands or a strong spoon.

Press half the mixture into a 2-litre baking dish or similar. Scatter over the pistachios and cranberries, then cover with the remaining meat mixture. Arrange the reserved bacon rashers over the top, tucking in the ends. Cover the dish tightly with foil, then put in a roasting tin. Pour boiling water into the tin to come halfway up the sides of the dish.

Bake for 60 minutes at 160 C, remove foil, then bake for 15 more minutes at 190 C to brown the bacon and make it golden. Cool completely, then wrap in fresh foil and chill. For the best flavour, let the terrine chill and mature for at least 2 days before eating.

This can also be frozen. Always allow to cool to room temperature before placing in the fridge or freezer. You can then defrost in the fridge for 24-36 hours before serving.

Chicken & Porcini Quenelle with Parmesan Black Pepper Cream Sauce

SERVINGS: 4-6

INGREDIENTS

30ml olive oil
1 large white onion, finely chopped
250g chicken breast finely shaved or diced
1 cup finely chopped mushroom OR use 20ml porcini dust
(blend down dehydrated mushroom)
5ml chicken stock powder
120 ml cream 40g flour or cornflour mixed to a paste with 40g soft butter
4 egg whites beaten to stiff peaks

METHOD

Boil 4 litres of salted water in a very large pot.

Heat the oil in a frying pan and add the onions, stir until cooked for about 3-5 minutes and then add the chicken sliced or diced, the porcini powder and seasoning.

Once the chicken has cooked add the cream, adjust the seasoning, add the butter and flour that has been mixed to a thick paste (beurre manie), cook through to thicken and then season to taste.

You can now blend to a thick paste in a food processor or blender. Once you have a smooth, delicious paste, fold in the stiff egg whites and fold in gently.

Spoon quenelle shapes of this glorious whipped chicken into the boiling water and poach for 1-2 minutes until cooked. Remove from boiling water with a slotted spoon and then place in a greased baking tray that is the correct size for this dish.

Find the Parmesan Pepper Cream Sauce in the sauces section of this book, page 153.

NOTE

You can change the flavour of this paste as often as you like:
- Add fresh lemon zest and, thyme, and black pepper
- Add fresh lime zest and chilli and coriander
- Add fresh sage and pink peppercorns
- Add saffron and lemon zest

Be as creative as you like!

Chorizo & Sweet Potato Croquettes

SERVINGS: 6-8

INGREDIENTS

100g chorizo sausage or bacon, finely chopped and cooked
2 cups mashed potato/sweet potato (you decide!)
3 tablespoons flour
1 egg + ½ cup breadcrumbs to bind
4 tablespoons parsley or herbs, finely chopped
1/2 cup grated cheese
salt and pepper to season
1-2 cups breadcrumbs or polenta to coat
oil for frying (or use air fryer and spray with oil)

METHOD

Combine chorizo/bacon, potato/sweet potato, cheese, flour, binding breadcrumbs, egg, and parsley together, then season to taste. Place a small amount of breadcrumbs in the bottom of a baking tray. Shape a tablespoon full of mixture into small logs (diameter about the size of a 10c coin and about 4cm long). Roll in breadcrumbs. Place coated croquettes in the baking tray.
Cover and refrigerate until ready to fry. You can use an air-fryer for these, but they would have to be done in a single layer.
Heat oil. Carefully place croquettes into the oil and cook until golden brown.
Remove and drain on a paper towel.

TO SERVE

Arrange croquettes on serving dishes, bling up and serve with Sugo sauce.

Easy Cheese Soufflés

Easy Cheese Soufflés

SERVINGS: 4-6

INGREDIENTS

1 tablespoon butter for greasing ramekins
1 tablespoon finely grated parmesan to coat ramekins
250 ml milk
30 g (¼ cup) flour mixed to a smooth paste with 30g butter (beurre manie)
125 g cheese (blue, cheddar, feta, parmesan etc)
4 eggs separated
1 pinch grated nutmeg
Salt and freshly ground pepper

METHOD

Heat the milk in a heavy-based saucepan until just bubbling around the edges. Now add the flour that has been mixed to a smooth paste with butter and whisk in. Continue to stir over medium heat until the sauce thickens.

Remove from heat and season to taste with salt and freshly ground pepper. Add cheese and the beaten egg yolks. While this is cooling, beat egg whites until really stiff and fold them into the cooled cheese sauce. Take care, not to over fold or you will lose volume and texture!!! I like to leave a few chunks of egg white just to make sure I don't overbeat.

Grease about 6 ramekin dishes with butter, and then coat with some finely grated Parmesan. This will help your soufflé 'climb' up the sides of the ramekin and get as high as possible. Now spoon the fluffy mixture into these ramekins to about ¾ full, and place in a roasting tray. Be gentle, don't bash these around. We always want to keep the precious air in that we whisked into the egg whites. Now, fill the roasting tray with about a quarter filled with cold water to make a Bain Marie.

Baking with steam will create a precious lift. Bake in a preheated oven of 190c for about 15 minutes, DEPENDING ON THE SIZE or until nice and risen and brown. Only take out when the tops look matt and are no longer glossy. It should smell heavenly!

Try to serve as quickly as you can once out of the oven. Remember, these will collapse shortly after they are removed from the oven as the steam will escape...so don't be too hard on yourself!

Glamourous Chicken & Cream Cheese Balls

SERVINGS: 4-6

INGREDIENTS

125 g cream cheese, softened
250-500 g chicken or turkey meat cooked and shredded (perfect for leftovers)
Zest of one lemon
1 cup chopped veg like broccoli, fennel, cauliflower,
green bean, capsicum, cabbage, celery, kale etc
1 teaspoon mustard
1 cup freshly chopped parsley, chives or similar

METHOD

Simply mix the cooked, cooled chicken or turkey with the cream cheese, zest, pepper, mustard, and veggies.
Stir to bind and then roll into balls.
Drop each ball into and through the chopped parsley and chives and ready to serve
on a starter platter, snack or quick, easy dinner!

Thai Fish Cakes

Thai Fish Cakes

SERVINGS: 4-6

INGREDIENTS

THAI FISH CAKES
- 1 garlic clove, smashed
- 3 Thai lime leaves cut into a DUST (finely chopped)
- 2 tablespoons coarsely chopped fresh coriander (root or leaves)
- 1 tablespoon fish sauce
- 500g firm white fish fillets such as ling, coarsely chopped
- 3 teaspoons of your fabulous curry paste
- Pinch of salt
- 3-5 snake or green beans, thinly sliced
- Peanut oil or coconut oil to shallow-fry

DIPPING SAUCE
- 1/4 cup white sugar
- 1/4 cup fresh lime juice
- 1 tablespoon fish sauce
- 1 finely chopped shallot
- ¼ cucumber, deseeded, finely chopped
- 1 small fresh red Birdseye chilli, deseeded, thinly sliced
- Kaffir lime leaves, chopped into a dust

METHOD

Place the cubed fish and garlic in the bowl of a food processor and process until finely chopped.

Add the lime leaves, coriander, fish sauce, curry paste, and salt, and process until just combined.

Transfer the fish mixture to a bowl.

Add the beans and stir to combine.

Divide the fish mixture into equal portions.

The best way to shape these is using wet hands to form thick patties.

Place on a plate on some greaseproof paper or chopping board.

Heat oil in a large frying pan until really hot. Cook patties on each side until light brown and cooked through. Transfer to a plate lined with a paper towel, repeat with the remaining patties, reheating the pan between batches.

DIPPING SAUCE

Combine the sugar, lime juice and fish sauce in a small saucepan over medium heat. Cook, stirring, for 5 minutes or until sugar dissolves. Remove from heat. Add the cucumber, shallot and chilli and stir to combine.

Serve hot or cold!

These fabulous fish cakes can be made the day in advance and then cooked closer to the time!

Enjoy!

Beef Carpaccio

SERVINGS: 4-6

INGREDIENTS

200g trimmed beef fillet
Juice and zest of two lemons
Extra virgin oil to drizzle
Salt and freshly ground pepper
Shaved Parmesan or Pecorino cheese

METHOD

Slice the beef fillets into thin medallions.
You can partially freeze the fillet first to make it easier to slice.
Place the medallions on a plastic chopping board (or similar) that has been brushed with olive oil.
Place another plastic sheet on top and beat with a mallet until paper thin.
Place the paper-thin slices of Carpaccio onto a large white plate.
Drizzle with lemon juice and zest. Drizzle with oil. Season. Then garnish with the cheese. I love Parmesan on my carpaccio, so this is like a Parmesan snow...or blizzard!

**You can also try this with capers, thinly sliced onions, and anchovies if you dare!
Or even fresh chillies.**

Rosemary Scented Egg Yolk Confit

INGREDIENTS

6 egg yolks, rinsed gently in water (much easier if they are fresh!); reserve the whites for meringues, pavlova or smoothies.

Olive oil or other, *enough to submerge the eggs in a heatproof dish*

Sprigs of rosemary or sage, or chilli to infuse the oil

METHOD

Simply rinse the egg yolks carefully and then place in the oil making sure the oil will cover the yolk completely.

Place in a preheated oven of 65c or use sous vide cooker and cook for about 10-12min. You will have to keep an eye on them so you do not overcook them. I use a slotted spoon to keep taking one of them out, checking how cooked it is, and then deciding how much longer they need. Remove gently and serve! Serve with carpaccio of beef, smoked or cured salmon, or prosciutto (or anything similar). Dress with micro herbs and petals and a matching sauce to drizzle

Steak Tartare

RECEIPT PER PERSON

INGREDIENTS

80- 100g beef fillet/tenderloin per person,
finely chopped with your sharpest chef's knife
1 small gherkin, finely chopped
1 tablespoon finely chopped red onion or shallot
1 teaspoon Dijon mustard
1 teaspoon Worcestershire sauce
½ teaspoon finely chopped capers
Freshly ground black pepper
Big pinch of salt to season
1 egg yolk (use my egg confit recipe on the precious page, or you can use a raw yolk)

METHOD

Simply chop the tenderloin into a fine dice; it will look almost as rough as store-bought mince.

Now add the remaining ingredients and stir through.
Adjust seasoning and stack in a stacking ring, OR simply arrange it on a sexy plate.

Make an indent on the top, and then position the egg yolk on top.
Garnish with micro herbs and petals, and serve!

Crispy Pork Spring Rolls

SERVINGS: 6-8

INGREDIENTS

FILLING

2 tablespoons vegetable/canola oil
2-3 cloves garlic (minced)
50g dried mung bean vermicelli noodles
(soak in water at room temperature for 8-10 minutes until soft, then drain)
80g julienne carrots
3 dried shiitake mushrooms (soaked until softened and thinly sliced)
75g white cabbage (julienne)
¼ cup Thai basil (roughly chopped)
¼ cup chopped coriander leaves
¼ cup thinly sliced spring onion
125g pork mince
2 tablespoons chicken stock
2 tablespoons oyster sauce
1 teaspoon cracked pepper

WRAPPING

1 pack of 8-inch square spring roll wrappers (total 20 sheets)
3 tablespoons of water
6 tablespoons of plain flour (to make the glue)
Canola oil (or peanut or vegetable oil for frying)

DIPPING SAUCE

1 cup white sugar
1 cup white vinegar
half teaspoon salt
2 tablespoons julienne carrots
4 large red chillis (de-seed, finely chopped)

METHOD

FILLING

Add 3 tablespoons of oil to a frying pan until hot. Add pork mince and cook over medium-high heat. After the pork has cooked about halfway, add the garlic mince and sliced mushrooms. Continue stir-frying for a few minutes until the pork is fully cooked. Put a colander over a stainless steel bowl, and then put the cooked pork mince into the colander and let it cool.

Use scissors to cut soft vermicelli noodles into 3 cm. long pieces and put them into a big bowl, then add julienne carrots, cabbage, basil, coriander, spring onion and cooked pork mince. Season the filling with chicken stock, oyster sauce, and cracked pepper. Wear gloves and massage all filling until well combined.

Mix together 3 tbsp. of water and 6 tbsp. of plain flour in a small bowl and use as glue for the spring roll wraps.

WRAPPING

Lay the wrapper on a flat surface by putting the triangle corner facing toward you. Put about two spoonfuls of the filling mixture onto the wrapper (about 2 inches from the corner that is closest to you).
Roll it over once and fold over both sides. Continue rolling it into a cylinder shape.
Use your finger/brush or small spoon to put the glue of mixed flour onto the corner end of the wrapper to seal it (making sure that the spring roll is tight but not overfilled so the it doesn't leak and burn when deep-frying).
Place all spring rolls onto a tray and leave a gap between them.
You can also freeze these spring rolls on the tray overnight and transfer them to a zip-lock bag when they are completely frozen for future use.

To fry the spring rolls, fill a small pot with oil until it's 2 to 3 inches deep. Heat the oil slowly over medium heat until it reaches 180-190c. Gently add the spring rolls one at a time, frying in small batches.
Carefully roll them in the oil so they cook evenly until golden brown, and transfer them to a plate lined with paper towels. Serve the spring rolls with the dipping sauce.

NOTE:
For vegetarian or vegan spring rolls, use the following ingredients:
- Vegan meat or tofu for pork mince
- Vegetable stock for chicken stock
- Soy sauce or vegan soy sauce for oyster sauce

DIPPING SAUCE

Put sugar, vinegar and salt in a small pot. Cook on medium heat until the sugar has dissolved.
Remove the pot from the heat and add 2 tbsp. of julienne carrots into the pot. Mix and put it aside.

Scented Beef & Basil Spring Rolls

SERVINGS: 4-6

INGREDIENTS

16 Spring roll sheets
Peanut, vegetable oil to brush the pastry
500 g lean beef mince
2 tablespoons or more curry paste
1 onion finely chopped (optional)
1/2 cup chopped basil and or mint
Fish sauce to season, or use stock if you prefer!

METHOD

Heat a greased frying pan and some vegetable oil up first until really hot, and then add the curry paste fry off to release the flavours. Now add the mince. Dry fry until brown, and then add the remaining ingredients. Allow to cook through; this mixture should be quite dry, but add some coconut cream if the mince is too lean. Season to taste with the fish sauce, and then add the herbs and allow to cool down.

Brush a piece of pastry, then place the filling in one corner and roll as per spring roll instructions. Roll up halfway, then fold in the flaps and continue rolling tightly and neatly. Brush with a little more oil and place on a baking sheet. Bake for about 15 minutes at 180°C until golden brown.

Serve baked spring rolls on a bed of lettuce and mint/basil leaves with sweet chilli sauce.

Mains

Eating is a necessity, but cooking is a celebration of life!

Mince with Pistachio & Date Gravel

Mince with Pistachio & Date Gravel

SERVINGS: 4-6

INGREDIENTS

2 squirts of a canola or rice bran cooking spray into a large non-stick pan
800g lean beef mince
(fluff this up with your hands so it's all nice and loose and fluffy and not in one big block)
1 large onion, finely diced
1 clove garlic crushed (optional)
1 tablespoon ras el hanout
(you can make your own using my recipe OR just use:
1 teaspoon cumin powder, 1/2 teaspoon cardamom powder and 1/2 coriander powder)
1 teaspoon turmeric
1/2 cup finely diced fennel, or you could use grated carrot, zucchini, or you choose!
1 tin chickpeas, drained & rinsed
1 cup chopped tomatoes or use one tin chopped tomato
2 tablespoons tomato paste or passata
1 vegetable or beef stock cube crumbled to a powder
Salt and pepper to season.
About 1 teaspoon of lemon zest

PISTACHIO & DATE GRAVEL

1-2 tablespoons pistachios bashed or chopped to a nice coarse gravel
2 tablespoons finely chopped dates
Lemon zest (1/2 teaspoon) and 1 tablespoon finely chopped parsley, mint or coriander for colour

Mince with Pistachio & Date Gravel

METHOD

The first thing you should do is heat and grease a large pan until just about smoking hot.
The mince MUST sizzle when it hits the pan.
Now add the mince that you have broken up in the packaging or a bowl so it is loose and fluffy already.
Put the mince into the pan…IT SHOULD SIZZLE nice and loud and sexy.

DO NOT STIR. I know you are worried about this burning and you are also worried about lumps, but let the mince brown and seal on the first side you put down FIRST and let the pan heat up again and THEN you can stir ever so slightly just to get some more mince onto the base of the pan.
My favourite mince 'fluffer' is one of those cheap plastic-coated whisks you get at the supermarket that only has about 4 loops. If you don't have one of those, use a strong plastic spoon or egg flip to break down the mince.

Once the mince is brown and fragrant and sexy ALL BY ITSELF, then and only then do you add the finely chopped onion and garlic. There should be enough oil out of the mince that you have rendered off during your amazing sizzle cooking of the mince at a nice high heat.
You can stir as much as you like now; by the way, that mince is SEALED off!

Now add the spices, stock powder and seasoning and stir through. Amazing colour, isn't it?

Finally, add the chopped tomatoes and, passata and chickpeas, and you're practically done.

Turn down the heat and let that all cook through, and then add the lemon zest, and it's ready to serve.

This way of cooking will not only save you time, BUT it will add valuable flavour and vibrant personality to your otherwise boring mince.
I love to get creative with my mince and change the spices, thus changing the flavour.

I served mine with a yoghurt swirl and the pistachio and date gravel with just a twist of fresh, peppery rocket leaves.

Moroccan Scented Mini Meat Loves with Cucumber & Cumin Dipping Sauce

SERVINGS: 4-6

INGREDIENTS

1 teaspoon olive oil
1 large onion finely chopped
1 clove garlic finely crushed
3ml turmeric powder
400g lean beef/pork/chicken minced
Salt and pepper to taste
Half a teaspoon of cumin or ras el hanout
Zest of one lemon or lime
1 whole egg beaten, seasoned and mixed with 125ml milk or lightly sour cream (light)

DIPPING SAUCE (just mix together and serve)

1 cup plain fat-free yogurt
Pinch of salt
large pinch cumin
2 tablespoons each cucumber and red onion

METHOD

These are wonderful to make in advance and then cook up as needed.

Fry the onions and the mince in a nice hot pan adding the turmeric and the garlic and the cumin/ras el hanout. When browned and fragrant, season to taste and then add the zest and juice of the lemon or lime. Place into the baking dish, and then pour the custard over the mince.
Bake for about 12-15 minutes until just done; these will cook faster in smaller dishes, so beware. Then, serve with the dipping sauce.

TO WRAP OR GARNISH
Zucchini ribbons slightly roasted (use your blowtorch or griddle pan)

Sexy Stir Fries

Sexy Stir Fries

SERVINGS: 4-6

INGREDIENTS

STIR FRY

1-2 tablespoons peanut/canola/sunflower/rice bran oil
600g chicken/pork/beef strips
1 cup zucchini, finely sliced or spiralized
1 cup carrots, finely sliced or spiralized
1 cup red onion, finely sliced.
2 cups finely sliced red or wombok cabbage
1 cup finely sliced red capsicum/red pepper
Peanut, chilli, and herb bling for crunch
1/2 cup peanuts, crushed and pan toasted
1-2 chopped fresh chillies, or use about half a teaspoon dried
1/2 cup freshly chopped mint/basil/coriander/cilantro

MARINADE

3 tablespoons honey or plum jam
3 tablespoons soy sauce
2 cloves garlic finely crushed
2 tablespoons crushed ginger
1-3 chillies finely chopped
2 drops sesame oil (optional)

METHOD

Remember! Your mission is to keep the sizzle up in your pan…if the pan goes quiet on you, you need to back away from the pan, get some of the pan naked, and then let the pan get back to temperature. HOT HOT HOT Swearword hot.

Put the marinade ingredients over the thin meat strips. Stir to combine.
Heat and grease the pan with the oil. When the pan is smoking hot, add the marinated chicken in a pile on one side of the pan. Please don't spread the meat over the pan; all that will do is smother the heat! Leave the meat in the pile until the first side of the meat that hit the pan, is beautifully brown and sexy and fragrant and sealed. You will need to have a sneaky look underneath one of the pieces using your tongs. Move that meat around by jiggling it with your tongs, but don't stir too much. Don't burn this! Keep checking! ONLY when that meat is brown underneath do you do a half stir so that some 'new' meat can hit the base of the pan? Keep doing this, keeping the sizzle high in the pan until all the meat has been perfectly browned. This way, your meat won't stew, and you can live happily ever after in the kitchen.

Once all the meat looks heavenly, sticky, and brown, start adding the vegetables on top. You can remove the meat from the pan if your pan is too small for all this action. Stir as much as you like now to get those vegetables hot and wilted right through. Check the seasoning and serve with rice, noodles, or just like that in a bowl with the heavenly peanut bling on top for valuable flavour and crunch!

Delectable Braised Duck with Spiced Carrot Purée

Delectable Braised Duck with Spiced Carrot Purée

SERVINGS: 4

INGREDIENTS

1 Whole Duck, trimmed

1 teaspoon Ras el Hanout/curry powder

1 teaspoon turmeric powder

Zest of one lemon or orange

Salt and pepper to season

Water to bind this paste

1 cinnamon quill, 1 star anise

2 litres of weak chicken stock

2 onions sliced or quartered

METHOD

Rub the duck with a paste made with water, dry spices and zest.

Rub into the skin of the duck and then add the remaining paste to the stock.

Place the stock, star anise, cinnamon and the onions into a baking tray and then add the duck breast side down.

Cook in a hot oven of 230c for about 45 minutes, then turn the duck over breast side up and cook for another 45 minutes. So your minimum cooking time here will be one and a half hours; if the duck is not yet tender (use a fork to test) reduce the heat of the oven to 160c and cook down for a further 15-30 minutes.

If the breast isn't quite brown enough, pop the grill on for about five minutes and watch closely!

Remove and carve and serve with the wonderful carrot purée in this book. Page 176.

Twice Cooked Sticky Plum & Ginger Pork Rashers

SERVINGS: 6-8

INGREDIENTS

800g-1kg pork rasher/pork or beef short rib
2 litres of liquid stock
1 tablespoon salt
2 star anise/cardamom pods
1 teaspoon cinnamon
2 teaspoons turmeric powder

STICKY PLUM AND GINGER GLAZE
Half cup plum jam
20ml crushed ginger
10ml crushed lemon grass
10ml crushed garlic
1 teaspoon turmeric
1/2 teaspoon salt

METHOD

Place the stock salt and spices in a large pot and then boil the pork rasher/pork or beef short rib hot and fast over high heat for at least 20 minutes.

Do not be alarmed! These will not look very appetizing once they are boiled, but this will soon be rectified once we add our delicious culinary glaze.

STICKY PLUM AND GINGER GLAZE

Remove the rashers from the boiling liquid and then drain. Place in a large bowl. Mix the jam with the crushed pastes and then stir through the rashers to coat them.

Place the rashers, single layer, in a greased roasting tray/baking dish and roast in a preheated oven of 200c for about 10-15 minutes until the rashers are golden and sticky. You can turn them over halfway, but if the oven is hot enough, they should seal from the heat of the tray as they roast.

You can also glaze these in your homemade BBQ sauce or a store-bought BBQ sauce or glaze.

Serve hot. Delicious.

Braised Pork Belly served on Caramelised Pear & Onion

Braised Pork Belly served on Caramelised Pear & Onion

SERVINGS: 8- 12

INGREDIENTS

2-4 cups weak chicken or vegetable stock (depending on the depth of the roasting dish)
2-4 kg pork belly
1 tablespoon turmeric
1 tablespoon cumin powder
or ras el hanout OR curry powder

2 onions thickly sliced for culinary high heels
2 bay leaves
2 star anise
2 tablespoons dark brown/raw/coconut/palm sugar
2 pears thickly sliced (no need to peel)

METHOD

To prepare the belly, ensure that you have dried the skin as much as possible. paper towel works well. Once the skin is dry you can even pop it under a fan to help dry the skin further. Season the skin with salt only at the very last minute. Place the belly into a shallow baking tray.

Pour the liquid, the onions, pears, and spices around the pork belly, taking special care not to wet the skin. If the belly is too low in places where the rib was taken out, prop it up with the onions and pears as 'high heels'. Season the skin with salt and then place in an oven, on the bottom rack of the oven, at 200c for about an hour and 15 minutes, keeping the liquid at least half way up the side of the pork the whole time. Then hike up the heat to about 230c for a further 20 minutes. Having the tray on the bottom shelf of the oven will help with your crackling later. If after the cooking time, your rind has not crackled, or only some of it has, feel free to leave the belly on the bottom shelf and turn on the grill. Having this direct heat on, with the tray at the bottom of the oven, means the grill can heat the rind, BUT NOT BURN IT. I call it a long-distance relationship with the grill, and the heat will help to crackle out the skin… every time. This is now your pork crackling superpower, and it will work every single time for you. Watch closely! Once the skin is brown and crisp, you can serve it with a stack of gorgeous vegetables or sides of your choice.

CHEFS NOTE

Pork belly does need time to be perfect. Time + heat = CRACKLING SUCCESS.
I can't wait for you to use the grill trick for many years to come.
If you can, once you have your crackling after the cooking time recommended above, hold for a further 30 minutes at 120 degrees C, making sure there is still braising liquid, and this will help tenderise thicker cuts of the belly. Enjoy.

Lamb Dishes

Lamb Backstrap with Pistachio Gravel

SERVINGS: 4

INGREDIENTS

800g lamb backstraps
SEASON WITH THE FOLLOWING SPRAY TAN:
1 teaspoon turmeric
50ml olive oil
Grated zest of one lemon
1 teaspoon dried thyme or oregano
Salt and pepper to season

GARNISH/BLING
4 teaspoons crushed pistachios toasted
4 teaspoons chopped dates
4 teaspoons chopped mint
4 teaspoons crumbled feta (optional)
1 teaspoon edible petals (optional)

METHOD

Season the backstrap with some turmeric, thyme, lemon zest, salt and olive oil.

Spray a non-stick pan with canola or rice bran oil and heat till nice and hot.

Now add the marinaded, spray-tanned lamb and cook for about 4 minutes on the first side and then turn. Repeat on the other side and then turn one more time.

This should give you a lovely medium pink lamb.

Rest the lamb, add all the bling ingredients together, then stir and serve.

In the photo, I have served this sliced, on a bed of the butterbean puree, with sexy vegetables and then the bling.

Fragrant Leg of Lamb with Turmeric & Cumin Rub, Served with a Dust of Pistachio & Petals

SERVINGS: 4

INGREDIENTS

1-1.2 kg leg of lamb deboned
1 tablespoon freshly grated turmeric
50 ml olive oil to drizzle
1 tablespoon Ras El Hanout

METHOD

Rub the lamb in all the above ingredients and allow it to rest.
Place the lamb skin side down in a hot frying pan and seal for about 4 minutes on each side until nicely sealed.
Place the lamb into a pre-heated oven of 200c for a further 15-20 minutes, depending on the size, and then remove and rest.
Carve and serve.

CUMIN AND PISTACHIO DUST

Roast 5ml cumin and then pound to a powder
Now roast half a cup of pistachios and grind lightly.
Add to the cumin powder and bulk up with petals and Nigella seeds, and use to garnish the lamb.

Fragrant Lamb Shoulder with Sticky Date, Pistachio & Lemon Gravel

Fragrant Lamb Shoulder with Sticky Date, Pistachio & Lemon Gravel

SERVINGS: 8-10

INGREDIENTS

2-4 kg-lamb shoulder bone in or out,
(but removed from trussing or netting & opened up)
Salt and pepper to season
1-2 litres of weak chicken stock
(this will depend on the depth of the baking dish)
1 teaspoon freshly grated turmeric (or powder)
1 tablespoon ground cumin/ras el hanout spice
1 cinnamon quill and 3 star anise

BLING
2 tablespoons chopped dried figs or pitted dates
Zest of one lemon
1/2 cup almonds/pistachios/other nuts roasted and chopped
1 tablespoon freshly chopped mint OR coriander

METHOD

Season the shoulder with salt and pepper, some of the turmeric and spices and rub into the skin with a little water or oil to give the shoulder a nice suntan.

Now place skin side up in a roasting tray with the stock, making sure the stock comes at least halfway up the shoulder so it is nicely submerged by half liquid.

Add the spices. If you have too much cooking liquid, reserve it for later, as you may need to top up the lamb during the cooking process.

Braising (roast with liquid) in a hot oven of 220c for at least an hour, remove from the oven and turn the shoulder over, return to the oven for half an hour and turn over again. Cook for another 15-30 minutes to get the skin nicely brown and crisp, and then remove from the oven.

BLING

Make the bling by mixing the chopped dates, nuts, herbs and zest together.
Garnish the lamb with the bling, and then serve!
NOTE: If you have a little more time, this actually benefits from a long slow cook, so reduce the heat to 160c and cook for 4 hours altogether! It will be falling apart with tenderness!

Steak Dishes

How to Cook the Perfect Steak

Often this is considered to be the greatest skill of the master chef.
Cooking a glorious steak is easy if you follow a few basic rules.

First of all, you need to choose the best steak you can afford for the occasion. Stay away from steaks that are sinewy and fatty. Favourites are fillet, porterhouse, rump, sirloin, or T Bone. These are all from the hindquarter and are considerably more tender than forequarter cuts.
Cook the meat at room temperature. Your pan should be heavy-bottomed so that it retains heat evenly and well.

Fry your steak in equal amounts of butter and vegetable oil. The butter will add flavour, while the vegetable oil will allow the right temperature to be achieved. Don't use one without the other. You can also just use canola cooking spray in a non-stick pan… works just as well without the extra calories!!

Always heat the pan with the butter and oil until swear-word hot BEFORE adding the steak. The steak should size and hiss. DO NOT STIR OR MOVE THE STEAK!!! Allow the meat to seal on the first side. Only turn over once the first side is perfectly brown (This is the side you should present up on the plate as
it will be the best side). This essential browning or searing of the meat is referred to as the Maillard reaction; not only is this a really cool cheffy term you can use to impress your friends and family, but using this method will instantly improve all your mince, chicken, and other meat dishes as browning meat (and veggies) makes them taste so much better.

If you have a thick-cut steak, I recommend turning a few times, as many as 8-12, to make sure you get the heat through your thick steak evenly. This is not necessary for steak under 3cm thick.
Once the first side is done, you can then turn the steak over and cook to the doneness you prefer.
Never press, poke or fiddle with the steak. Rather, leave the juices inside, where they belong.

Checking for doneness – this is truly the most important part. Many steaks are ruined by overcooking. Remember, the steak will continue to cook as it rests… very important, or the steak will be ruined.

Steak Done-ness Test

A practiced poke with your finger and you will eventually be able to judge the approximate doneness of your steak. Use the following as a guide but experience is the best teacher.

DONE-NESS	DESCRIPTION	INTERNAL TEMP
VERY RARE	Feels soft and squishy. You can feel it's totally raw.	26-28 degrees C
RARE	Soft and yielding to the touch. Like poking your cheek with your finger	49-51 degrees C
MEDIUM	Yields gently to the touch. Like poking your chin on the fleshiest part.	55-57 degrees C
MEDIUM-WELL	Yields only slightly to the touch, beginning to firm up, again like your chin would feel if you pressed with your finger.	60-63 degrees C
WELL-DONE	Hard to the touch, does not give way.	71 degrees C & over

Resting

Now for the most important part... don't serve it straight away. Let the steak 'rest' for about 4 minutes, depending on the thickness. This allows the juices to move back into the meat.

Resting should be done in a place that is about room temperature and with only a loose covering over the meat. If you doubt me, try cutting a steak in half right off the grill. Let a second one rest for 5 minutes and then cut into it. See which one is juicier.

Sous Vide Sexy Black Steak with Juniper & Black Salt Rub

INGREDIENTS

120-250g rump, sirloin, tenderloin or pork chop per person.
Season each piece with salt and pepper, or use a fancy mis or black salt flakes, some crushed juniper or sage, and peppercorns of your choice.

METHOD

Pre-heat pot or reheat the sous vide bath to 52°C / 126°F for a rare-medium- rare (see DONENESS CHART on the previous page for doneness preference).

Season your steaks on all sides with either just salt and pepper or a mixture of powdered juniper and black salt. Seal your steaks by using a vacuum sealer or just pop them in a zip lock bag. Cook sous vide at 50c for rare, 55c for medium rare and 60c for medium doneness for 60 minutes for 2.5 cm thick cuts.

Remove the steaks from the bags and pat them dry. Sear the outside of the steaks either in a hot pan with equal amounts of butter and vegetable oil OR I find a blowtorch to be a practical and entertaining way to sear. Mind those hands and eyebrows!

Once you have cooked your sous vide steaks to perfection in your pan, and they are resting for about 4-5 minutes, simply build this sauce using the SAME pan (provided you didn't burn anything) and simply add the Truffle Sauce Ingredients in the recipe set out below to create an amazing quick and easy one pan sauce for your steak. Always check your seasoning; it shows you care.

Fillet with Porcini & Sage Cream

SERVINGS: 4

INGREDIENTS

1 tablespoon canola oil to heat in the pan to sear the beef
4 cloves garlic, minced
4 shallots finely chopped
1 cup porcini or your favourite mushroom finely chopped
1 teaspoon freshly chopped sage or thyme
1 chicken/mushroom or vegetable stock cube
50-80ml cream

METHOD

Heat the oil in a saucepan over medium-low heat. Add the garlic and shallots and cook for 5 minutes, stirring, being careful not to burn them, but browning them will be perfect.

Add the mushrooms, the sage, the stock cube, and the cream and then stir through and let heat through and boil for about a minute. Serve with the steak.

SEXY BLACKENED FILLET

Rub approximately 150-200g portions of beef fillet in sexy black salt flakes or normal flake salt and black pepper to coat.
Cook hot and fast as per previous instructions, and then serve with the porcini cream.

Seafood Dishes

Creamy Sherry & Garlic Mussels

Creamy Sherry & Garlic Mussels

SERVINGS: 4

INGREDIENTS

1 kg mussels
15ml butter and 15ml vegetable oil
1 large onion finely diced
2 cloves garlic, crushed
80ml sweet sherry
500ml chicken or vegetable stock
125ml fresh cream
80g pecorino or parmesan finely grated
2 tablespoons chopped chives or parsley

METHOD

Heat and grease a frying pan, and then add the butter and oil.
Stir fry the garlic, onion, and herbs for about a minute or two and then add the sherry.
Allow to boil until the sherry has reduced by half.
Add the stock and then the mussels, and place a lid on the pot.
Steam through for 5-8 minutes, and then add cream and pecorino. Season to taste and serve.

Scampi/Prawns Poached in Burnt Almond & Sage Butter

SERVINGS: 4

INGREDIENTS

350g prawn or scampi meat, cleaned and prepared
125g butter
2 tablespoons almond slivers/shaved
3-4 fresh sage leaves, torn
1 tablespoon almond liquor

METHOD

Simply melt the butter over medium heat; once it starts to bubble, add the prawn/scampi meat and cook through; this should only take a minute or two, depending on the size of the flesh.
The butter should bubble and go a very light caramel brown.
Now add the almond liqueur and flambe. Remove from heat and serve.

Snapper Baked with Nam Jim or Chiang Mai

Snapper Baked with Nam Jim or Chiang Mai

SERVINGS: 4-6

INGREDIENTS

1.2 kg whole snapper or barramundi (approx 250g per person)
Sliced spring onions or fried shallots to garnish
CHOOSE ONE OF THESE SAUCES

CHIANG MAI CURRY PASTE
- ½ teaspoon salt
- 3 big red chillies (or as you prefer)
- 2 tablespoons Ginza (ginger) skin removed, chopped
- 2 tablespoons lemongrass chopped
- 2 shallots chopped
- 1 garlic clove chopped
- 1 teaspoon shrimp paste
- 1 tablespoon turmeric, fresh or dried

NAM JIM SAUCE
- Half cup fresh coriander/use roots too
- 2 teaspoons minced ginger
- 1-3 red and or green chilli (use more if you like!)
- 60ml fresh lime juice
- 30-45 ml fish sauce (balance to your preferred taste; I like mine saltier)
- 1 tablespoon palm or brown sugar
- 1 cup red onion chopped
- 1 tablespoon peanut/avocado or vegetable oil
- 3 tablespoons chopped mint

METHOD

CHIANG MAI CURRY PASTE

Put all the ingredients in a mortar and pestle or in a stick blender until it forms a smooth, thick paste.

NAM JIM SAUCE

Place into a food processor or blender and simply whizz together.

SNAPPER

Place your fish in a baking tray and then smother it in the sauce you have chosen from the recipe above. (use what you need and freeze the rest), Make sure you cover the fish with sauce inside and out, and then season lightly with salt.

Place in a hot oven of 220c for 20- 25 minutes until brown and delicious. Test if the thickest part is cooked by flaking it with a fork.

Garnish with the shallots of sliced spring onions and serve.

CHEF'S NOTE

To fry your fish Asian style, simply coat the fish in a mix of even amounts of plain flour and cornflour, dust off the excess, fry in hot vegetable oil for 4-6 minutes until golden and cooked and then serve with the nam jim sauce and your shallot or spring onion garnish.

Seared Crispy Skin Fish with Pancetta Bark & Rustic Pea Mash

Seared Crispy Skin Fish with Pancetta Bark & Rustic Pea Mash

SERVINGS: 4

INGREDIENTS

CRISPY SKIN FISH

500-800g fish, skin on
Salt and pepper to season
Half lemon or lime per serving
4-6 strips of Pancetta placed on a roasting tray and then baked until crispy in a hot oven of 200°C

RUSTIC PEA PURÉE

2 cups frozen peas
1 onion finely chopped
1 clove garlic minced
150 ml chicken or vegetable stock
(depending on thickness required - please adjust)
20g butter
80 cream

METHOD

This is my favourite recipe for when I am entertaining because it is practically stress-free! A beautiful piece of fish or salmon needs little masking and, if cooked perfectly, will simply shine.

The trick is to cook the fish properly and get the skin sexy and crispy. You need to get your pan or BBQ SWEAR WORD HOT and greased with about 5 ml vegetable or rice bran oil in the pan just so that the fish doesn't stick. I have also started doing this in the air fryer for about 8 minutes, then removing the skin, then cooking for a further 5 minutes.

When the pan is hot, place the fish (not skin side) presentation side down, and use your tongs to make sure it doesn't stick…I just give the piece a little wiggle to make sure it hasn't stuck, but it will create a sexy crust of flavour and colour.

When the first side is brown (simply look underneath and lift with your tongs), turn it over to do the skin side, too. After about a minute or two, you should be able to remove the skin using the tongs. Don't stress if it breaks or you have to strip-peel it off; it is all part of the rustic glamour of this dish. Place the skin aside and then turn the now skin-free side down to brown it off.

When the fish is cooked (check by placing a fork or knife in the centre of the thickest part, and if it flakes when you twist, it is done.)

Remove from the pan, lower the heat, and fry the skin nice and hot but not so hot that it burns in a flash…this will dry and crisp up the skin, and the best way is to remove the skin so you don't overcook the fish! NEVER serve soggy fish skin…it is just not glamorous and can be easily crisped up by just allowing it some alone time in the pan.

Serve with this amazingly versatile pea puree. Don't like peas? Use butterbeans (drained out of a tin) instead.

RUSTIC PEA PURÉE

Place all the ingredients into a medium saucepan and boil over medium heat until just heated through, about 3-5 minutes. Remove from the heat and blend to a smooth puree with a stick blender or manual masher. Adjust the seasoning and thickness, and then serve

Giant Tiger Prawns with Peri Peri

Giant Tiger Prawns with Peri Peri

SERVINGS: 2-4

INGREDIENTS

1kg giant tiger prawns
2 onions, finely chopped
6 cloves garlic, minced
10 Birds Eye Chillies
1 cup lemon juice. Fresh juice only. Never long life.
zest of one lemon
1 cup olive oil
1 teaspoon salt
1 teaspoon sugar
2 tablespoons hot or sweet paprika
Lemons halves to serve, blacken cut side in a hot pan.

METHOD

Clean and devein the prawns by cutting down the back of the prawn with a good pair of kitchen scissors and removing the vein. Keep the shell on. You can cut almost right through the prawn to butterfly them OR just leave them whole.

Pop all the other ingredients into a food processor and whizz until it forms a thick, fragrant paste, or you can chop it the good old-fashioned way. Now, use this sauce to marinate your prawns.

To cook the prawns in their lovely sauce, simply heat your greased pan or outside on the BBQ or coal fire to a good but medium heat and then place the prawns, flesh side down, and get them nicely browned and sealed off before turning over and browning the shell. They don't take long, so please don't overcook!

Serve with lemon halves that have been blackened in a hot pan on the cut side.

Tea Smoked Crispy Skin Salmon

SERVINGS: YOU DECIDE

INGREDIENTS

Cooking oil or spray (not olive)
80-100g salmon per person, with skin
salt and pepper to season
1/2 cup black or rooibos tea leaves
1/2 cup rice, any kind
1 teaspoon cumin or coriander seeds
2-3 star anise, cardamom or cinnamon (you choose)

METHOD

Grease the colander or rack with the oil or cooking spray.
Place the seasoned fish pieces skin side up on the rack.
Place the rice, tea and spices in the pan and then put the fish on the rack on top.
Close with a lid. Place on full heat. When you see smoke, THEN time for 15 minutes.
The fish will cook when the hot smoke starts to circulate.
When 15 minutes is done, take the pot/pan OUTSIDE and remove the lid.
Remove the skin using tongs, and place on a greased baking tray.
Pop under the preheated grill or in a hot oven at 200 C until the skin is crispy and perfect.
Serve with pea puree, caramelised lemon and crispy skin.
Perfect and so quick and easy and healthy.

CHEF'S NOTE:

You will need a pot that can fit a cake rack or colander inside, with a tight-fitting lid
OR a deep frying pan with a lid and a cake rack that can fit inside
You MUST have a close-fitting lid.

Spectacular Paella Made Easy

SERVINGS: 6-8

INGREDIENTS

1 large onion finely sliced

3-6 cloves garlic

3 tablespoons olive oil

Pinch saffron threads, soak in 30ml boiling hot water, allow to seep

1 teaspoon turmeric

1 tablespoon paprika (sweet or smoked)

2-3 teaspoons chicken stock powder

OR 2 stock cubes mixed into 1L boiling hot water. OR use 1L prepared chicken stock

12-16 prawns whole or peeled tail on (optional)

substitute with 12-16 chipolata sausages if you want!

12-16 scallops roe off (optional, omit if you prefer)

800g chicken pieces skin on *OR skin-free chicken strips*

2-3 chorizo sausages, sliced (you can never add too many of these!)

12-16 gorgeous mussels (green lip or your favourite)

350g medium grain rice

1 green capsicum cut into strips, seeds removed

1 red capsicum cut into strips, seeds removed

200g button or brown mushrooms

1 tablespoon butter

2 lemons

Fresh parsley and edible petals for garnish (optional)

METHOD

Spray a Paella pan or large frying pan big enough to cook for 6-8 people with canola cooking spray. Put over the heat and allow the pan to get nice and hot! I call this swear word hot, so you know how hot I want it. Getting the pan nice and hot will help you to brown everything beautifully, which will add beautiful flavour and personality to the dish. Stewed grey food does not taste sexy!

Add 1 tablespoon of the olive oil and allow to heat, and then add the chorizo slices; they should sizzle nice and hot as they hit the pan. Only stir once the first layer that hits the pan has browned off nicely. Stir a little to brown off most of the chorizo, and then add the chicken pieces into the fat that will render off the chorizo. This will help the chicken pieces or strips brown up and get valuable flavour. Please don't stir too much; keep the sizzle up in the pan at ALL TIMES!

Turn occasionally and make sure nothing burns; it's all about managing the heat in the pan. A nice even sizzle during the entire browning phase is optimal! Step away from the pan if you're a compulsive stirrer! But also don't allow it to burn! Once most of the chicken and chorizo are browned, it doesn't have to be fully cooked through at this stage. Add the onions, turmeric, paprika, and garlic and stir through to cook until tender and the spices are fragrant. Remove this mixture from your pan into a big bowl and return the pan to the heat. Now allow the pan to heat up 1 Tablespoon of the olive oil and brown the prawns (optional) and scallops (optional) on both sides in a nice sizzling hot pan.

If you aren't using seafood, I suggest adding delicious little chipolata sausages. Instead, those could go in with the chicken and chorizo though, but with the seafood, you are best to have a swear word hot EMPTY pan so they brown off beautifully and don't stew in an overcrowded pan. Once seafood/sausages are cooked, add to the chicken chorizo mix and set aside. We will add these back into the pan in a minute or two!

Now add 1 tablespoon of the olive oil, and when hot, add the rice (dry and raw) into the oil and stir to coat; add the capsicum strips and mushroom and then the stock. Add the saffron threads and their yellow water. The stock should cover the rice mixture and be full of flavour even at this stage. Now add all the chicken and, prawn and chorizo mix back over this rice mixture, all that lovely flavour with cook through into your rice.

Reduce the heat and make sure that all of your rice is below the liquid line; if not, just use a spoon to dip it under, or else it WON'T COOK! Allow to cook over this low heat for about 20 minutes; you can partially cover it with a big lid. You must cook over low heat, or else this will burn instead of making the sexy and delicious Paella 'crust' where the rice brownies form a delicious layer. The crust is called the SOCARRAT.

After 20 minutes, test some of the rice; it should be nice tender, and tasty.

Adjust the seasoning as necessary, and then also check if you have chicken pieces if you've used them, and have cooked through them. You can add a little more liquid if your liquid has completely cooked away and the rice still is sheer. Add the mussels, put the lid back on, and let them steam for about 5-10 minutes.

When the mussels are done, you are ready to serve; squeeze one lemon over the gorgeous dish, garnish with parsley and the petals, and serve. I was ready before my guests were, so I popped the whole Paella pan into the oven at about 80 degrees C just to hold it until they were ready.

Chicken Dishes

Sage Infused Sweet Potato & Speck Hot Rubbed Spatchcock with Ras El Hanout Spray Tan

SERVINGS: 6

INGREDIENTS

3 Spatchcock's OR 1 large chicken
1 quantity of Sweet Potato and Speck stuffing

SWEET POTATO AND SPECK STUFFING
2 cups roasted sweet potato
1 cup speck (or bacon), diced
2 small onions, chopped
2 cloves garlic
50-100g feta, goats cheese or ricotta
1 teaspoon sage, chopped

SPRAY TAN
1 teaspoon turmeric powder
1 teaspoon ras el hanout OR curry powder
30ml Oil
Salt
Pepper

METHOD

To make the stuffing – cook the speck in a swearword hot pan, not stirring until it has started browning.
Add the onion and garlic and cook through.
Remove from heat and add the cooked mashed sweet potato, cheese and sage.
Mix to combine, season and set aside.
Cut spatchcock down the back – just to the side of the backbone.
Place bird skin side up on a breadboard, head and neck side closest to you. Now start loosening the skin off the breast meat and work all the way under the skin; loosen the skin on the thighs and legs of the bird, making an envelope and stuff with the sweet potato mixture.
Stray tan the bird with the turmeric mixed with some oil. Roast in a hot oven (200°C) for about 20 minutes until cooked through.

TO SERVE
Cut each spatchcock in half and serve with cauliflower puree and steamed green beans and zucchini in a lemony, buttery sauce, topped with pistachio crumbs, black salt, petals and micro-herbs.

Tarragon & Porcini Stuffed Spatchcock

SERVINGS: 4-6

INGREDIENTS

3 x 480g Spatchock birds or use 1 large chicken
2 cups fresh sourdough
breadcrumbs OR 2 cups fresh cauliflower
2 large onions finely chopped
80g porcini mushrooms
2 cloves garlic
3 tablespoons freshly chopped
tarragon/marjoram/thyme
3 tablespoons melted butter
1 tablespoon flake salt and some oil

METHOD

Make the sourdough or cauliflower crumbs by blending in a food processor until very fine. Add the mushrooms, herbs, garlic and butter and salt and process. You should have lovely, fragrant crumbs. Cut the bird down the backbone on 1 side of the spine and then turn over and flatten, breaking the breast bone.

Using your fingers, loosen the skin off the flesh to create a neat little pocket all the way down to the drumsticks and thighs. Use a tablespoon to shove the stuffing under the skin on top of the flesh right down to the drumsticks and thighs and over the breasts. You will need to share the stuffing between the birds. Once stuffed, reshape the bird and then rub it with the oil and salt to season.

Bake in a preheated oven of 220c for about 15-20 minutes until the birds have a lovely 'suntan' and are cooked through.

Tea Poached Asian Spatchcock with Fresh, Hot & Sexy Salad

SERVINGS: 4-6

INGREDIENTS

POACHING

- 1.2-1.8 kg whole chicken (or use duck, spatchcock or quail)
- 2 cloves garlic
- 2-3 star anise
- 2 teaspoons ginger
- 1 tablespoon turmeric (chicken bronzer!)
- 1 onion finely chopped OR 5 small red shallots
- 50 ml Shaoxing rice wine
- 1 cinnamon quill
- ¼ cup tea leaves
- Peel of one orange or tangerine
- 1 teaspoon Pink or Sichuan peppercorns
- 2-3 litres chicken stock
- 50 ml Mirin

SALAD

- 1 pear or apple julienne
- 1 small fennel julienne
- 1 red onion finely chopped
- 1 cup red cabbage/beetroot finely chopped
- 2 tablespoons plain yogurt or crème fraiche
- Lettuce, spinach, beetroot leaves
- Edible petals (optional)
- Pinch of turmeric
- 1 chopped chilli
- Juice of one lime
- Teaspoon poppy seeds
- 1 tablespoon roasted and chopped nuts (Pistachio or pine)

METHOD

POACHING

Place all the ingredients for the poaching (NOT THE SALAD INGREDIENTS) in a large pot, big enough that the liquid can cover the chicken. Simply bring to a simmer and then allow to cook through for at least an hour until tender. Remove from the heat and then strain to just retain the liquid; place the liquid back in the pot and cook hot and fast to reduce the liquid to about a litre or until it's concentrated enough to provide a good broth or soup for later! You get two dishes out of this recipe isn't that fabulous!

SALAD

For the salad, simply mix it all together – simple.
Once the bird is cool enough to handle, chop or shred and then serve on a bed of the fabulous hot, fresh and sexy salad.

Coq Au Vin Featuring Spatchcock served with Fragrant Mash

SERVINGS: 6-8

INGREDIENTS

3 spatchcock quartered

250 ml red wine

250 g bacon diced

20 pickling onions

250 g mushrooms

3 cloves garlic crushed

2 onions chopped

1 cup good chicken stock

4 tablespoons tomato paste 2 sprigs thyme or

1 teaspoon dried

TO THICKEN

¼ cup flour mixed to a paste with 2 tablespoons soft butter

METHOD

Fry the spatchcock/chicken pieces skin down in a REALLY hot pan.
Add the bacon and allow to brown.

Now add the mushrooms, onions and wine and allow the wine to cook away.
Add the garlic and the remaining ingredients and allow to cook gently for about 15 minutes or until the baby onions are soft.

To thicken the sauce, whisk the butter and flour paste into the sauce with a whisk until thick and glossy.
Serve with mashed potatoes and/or croutons.

Home Smoked Chicken Mayo & Mint Gourmet Stacks

Home Smoked Chicken Mayo & Mint Gourmet Stacks

SERVINGS: 6-8

INGREDIENTS

200g smoked chicken breast fillets, sliced thinly (use smoked salmon if you prefer!)

50ml -100ml fat-free yogurt

1 tablespoon freshly chopped mint and/or basil

1 granny smith apple, cored and finely sliced

Half a cup fennel, julienne

1 cup finely chopped broccoli

Lots of ground black pepper

1 teaspoon grainy mustard

1 cucumber, make into ribbons using your peeler

(or slightly roast zucchini ribbons instead)

Slices of roasted sweet potato, lightly coated in your favourite spice… be creative!

METHOD

Place the sweet potato on a large white platter or individual dinner plates.

Mix the chicken, yogurt, fennel, mint and apple together and mix.

Place a large tablespoon of this in the centre of the sweet potato.

Now use a cucumber or zucchini ribbon to wrap around the filling to create a neat little stack….easy! And so gorgeous!

Now garnish with lots of ground black pepper and fresh rocket or mustard cress, and serve! Drizzle with herbed oil if you're feeling daring!

TO SMOKE THE CHICKEN OR SALMON

Place the chicken or salmon seasoned on a rack.

The rack needs to fit into a pot or wok and keep the chicken or salmon off the base.

Put about 6 tablespoons either tea, lavender or wood sawdust or half a cup of smoke on the base of the pan or wok and then put the lid on and smoke hot and fast for about 12 minutes.

Remove the skin of the salmon and crisp in the oven.

To get the chicken to smoke faster, simply butterfly.

Vegetable Dishes

'Learn how to cook - try new recipes, learn from your mistakes, BE FEARLESS! Most of all - have fun!' - Julia Child

Cauliflower Paella

SERVINGS: 4 - 6

INGREDIENTS

10ml oil or cooking spray

450-600g chicken pieces of your choice

cut into pieces no larger than your palm (optional; you can keep this vegetarian)

80g chorizo sausage or bacon, finely diced or minced *(optional)*

1 onion, minced or finely chopped

1 head cauliflower, food processed (cauliflower rice)

1 tablespoon smoked or sweet Paprika

1 teaspoon ground turmeric

1 teaspoon garlic paste

1 teaspoon chicken stock powder

Juice and zest of one lemon

1 cup peas, snow peas or beans

80g fire-roasted capsicum (from your deli)

Pinch of dried or 1 teaspoon of fresh sage or thyme

METHOD

Spray a large nonstick frying pan with cooking spray or oil and allow the pan to get swearword hot.

Once hot, add the chorizo gravel/mince and allow to brown nicely. Don't stir just for fun; only stir if it needs to be stirred. We want the sausage to render its fat, and if you cool it down too much, it will stew. Now add the onions, garlic, and herbs and cook through. You can reduce the heat at this stage.

Coat the chicken in the spices and the stock powder to give it a Spanish spray tan. Make some space in the pan, turn the heat up, and add the chicken to the hot pan. Don't stir until the first layer of chicken is brown, then stir and turn the pieces to brown.

Once browned, add the capsicum, peas, cauliflower rice and lemon zest, and stir fry until tender. Season to taste, and then add the lemon juice! Ready to serve! So quick and easy.

Truffled Mushroom Pizza with Cauliflower Sweet Potato Topping

SERVINGS: 4-6

INGREDIENTS

4-6 large brown mushrooms wrapped in greased foil to protect them in the oven
1 cup cauliflower mash
(simply simmer cauliflower in milk and/or stock until tender, season and then mash)
1 cup roasted sweet potato slices
2 tablespoons truffle/lemon/orange oil (from a deli or supermarket)
Salt and pepper to season
, Parmesan cheese finely grated on zester to make Parmesan snow

METHOD

Top the mushroom with the roasted sweet potato and then the cauliflower, drizzle with the oil and then garnish with the cheese, bake for about 10-12 minutes until done - delicious!

Sexy Roast Vegetables

Sexy Roast Vegetables (not the pale soggy ones!)

SERVINGS: 2-4

INGREDIENTS

1 cup diced sweet potato
1 cup diced cauliflower
1 cup diced carrot
1 cup diced beetroot
1 cup diced potato
1 cup diced pumpkin

METHOD

Place on a tray and then drizzle with extra virgin olive oil, your choice of spices, salt and pepper. Not too much; these don't need to be drowned or over-spiced; they will be sexy just with a little love.

Cook in a SWEAR WORD HOT oven (220C) for 35 minutes, less if your dice is smaller.
You can use any combination of vegetables that you have available to you.

I always add some green veg after I've roasted the sexy veggies to add some colour and texture.
I steam either beans, snow peas, broccoli or asparagus and then add to the mix.

You can then serve these with a main course or on their own with either a pea puree or chickpea/butter bean mash to hold the stack together.

CHEF'S NOTE

Always go for colour! Some veggies are better for roasting, and some are better for steaming. These veggies are BETTER roasted swear word hot and fast at 220C...this amount of veggies in an oven of 180C will throw SO much steam that they will NEVER go brown.

So, crank the oven up to swear word hot so that we get LOTS of colour in these veggies. When vegetables are roasted they caramelise and give 100% more flavour and personality than when steamed.
I do about a 3cm dice, but you can go bigger or smaller. The larger they are, the longer they will take to cook.

Gourmet Sweet Potato & Cauliflower Mash

SERVINGS: 4-6

INGREDIENTS

½ head cauliflower, finely cut to make 'rice'
2 potatoes, peeled and finely diced
5ml cumin powder
2 teaspoons chopped parsley or chives
Salt and pepper to season
100ml soured cream/cream/ milk to bind
250ml chicken or vegetable stock

METHOD

So simple. Place everything in a pot except the cream and herbs. Cook over medium heat until the potato and cauliflower are tender. Remove from heat. Add the cream and then mash to form a smooth, delicious mash, then add in the herbs, season and serve.

Quick Sweet Potato Curry

SERVINGS:

INGREDIENTS

1 tablespoon curry paste
250ml coconut cream (or coconut milk)
2 cups cooked sweet potato (very small cubes)
1 teaspoon shredded lime leaves
Zest and juice of one lime
Fish sauce to season
Coriander to garnish

METHOD

Heat the coconut cream or milk with your curry paste and bring to a boil to release the flavours. Now add the sweet potato and cook over low heat until the sweet potato is soft. Add the lime leaf shreds, zest, fish sauce and juice, as well as the seasoning to taste.

TIP
You could also roast this dish instead of doing it over the stovetop!

TO SERVE
Serve garnished with chopped coriander and even caramelised limes.

Sexy Petit Pois
Peas with Bacon Cream Sauce a la Le Troquet

SERVINGS: 4-6

INGREDIENTS

500 g frozen petit pois (baby peas) 100g diced bacon, pancetta or Serrano ham

1 onion finely chopped

100ml cream

100ml chicken, vegetable or mushroom stock liquid

METHOD

When I was still a student, I had the pleasure of working at a gorgeous family-owned French restaurant in Durban, South Africa, called Le Troquet. The popular restaurant traded for 29 years, and I was lucky enough to work there over a five-year period while I studied, worked and travelled. I was practically part of the family and still am friends with Gilbert and Annick, the owners. **They have since retired, but their peas live on…**

Heat a non-stick pan with a little canola spray or just a drizzle of oil… I really mean just a smidgen.

When the pan is swear word hot, add the bacon, pancetta or ham that has been finely diced. Fry until brown and delicious (don't stir too much, as this will encourage the pan to cool down, and the bacon will lose its personality and flavour).

Once the bacon is sexy and brown, add the onion/garlic, which has been finely chopped, and stir through until soft. Add the peas, the stock and the cream and allow the liquid to heat and cook the peas. About 8-12 minutes. Adjust the seasoning with salt and pepper, and then serve.

The Art of Making Stock

Stocks are much less intimidating than they appear to be. Yes, it's easier to buy a stock cube, and also, it's a big commitment in fridge and freezer space making your own stock, but it's definitely worth it if you have the time and the space to store them.

Chicken Stock

INGREDIENTS

1 whole chicken
1.250 litres water
1 large white or brown onion, quartered with skin on or off
2 large carrots peeled and roughly chopped
1 leek roughly chopped
1 stick celery chopped
1 teaspoon black peppercorns
Bouquet Garni (6 parsley on the stalk, 6 thyme stalks, 3 bay leaves) tied together with cooking-grade string.
1 teaspoon salt

METHOD

Place all of the ingredients in a large pot; you can either leave the bird whole or cut it up to fit.
Slowly bring this to the boil and then simmer, with a lid, for about an hour to two hours.
Remove from the heat, and allow to cool on the bench for 30 minutes or until cool enough to handle.
Remove the larger pieces and then strain through a sieve, reserving the strained liquid in a suitable container.
You can blot the oil on the surface with a bit of paper towel if you prefer.
Use immediately, or store in an airtight container in your fridge for up to four days or in the freezer for up to 3 months.
Always adjust the seasoning to suit your dish.
Use the chicken shredded or chopped up in salads, pasta, etc; it will be just gorgeous.

Simple Beef/Bone Stock

INGREDIENTS

500g marrow bones/beef shin or similar bone in
1 onion quartered
2 carrots, roughly chopped
1 large stick celery, chopped
Bouquet Garni (6 parsley on the stalk, 6 thyme stalks, 3 bay leaves) tied together with cooking-grade string.
1 teaspoon peppercorns
1 teaspoon salt
1.250 litres water

METHOD

Preheat a large frying pan.
When hot, brown the beef/bones on each side. DO NOT STIR TOO MUCH at this stage; stir just enough to keep them from burning. If you have liquid coming off the bones, chances are you are stirring too much and cooking the pan, making the bones stew instead of brown. Keep the heat up so that you have a constant sizzle of heat from the pan. The heat needs to remain up to help brown the bones. The brown from the bones will be where the flavour comes from.
Now, place all of the ingredients, including the browned bones, in a large pot.
Slowly bring this to the boil and then simmer, with a lid, for about an hour to two hours.
Remove from the heat, and allow to cool on the bench for 30 minutes or until cool enough to handle.
Remove the larger pieces and then strain through a sieve, reserving the strained liquid in a suitable container. You can blot the oil on the surface with a bit of paper towel if you prefer.
Use immediately, or store in an airtight container in your fridge for up to four days or in the freezer for up to 3 months. Always adjust the seasoning to suit your dish.

Basic Sauces

ALL SAUCE RECIPES MAKE A SERVING SIZE OF 4-6

Knowing your way confidently around some really sexy traditional sauces will make you so much cheffier.

NOTE FROM CHEF MEL:

Having a reliable repertoire of amazing sauces to complement your dishes is so exciting and delicious. These are some classical French Style sauces, as well as some Italian and global influences.
I hope you have as much fun saucing from a pan as much as I do! Make sure you get a photo of you saucing from the pan; it's a very cheffy shot.
It's like the crowning glory, food makeup or accessory for your perfect dish.

Roux is the liaison of butter and flour to thicken sauces at the beginning of the cooking process. The Roux forms the base of many sauces, including Béchamel and Velouté.

You can also thicken sauces, soups and gravies at the end of the cooking process by doing a **'reverse roux',** which is equal amounts of butter and flour, mixing them together to a paste, and then whisking in (off the heat) at the end, cook through once and then it will thicken the sauce.

You could also thicken it with arrowroot or cornflour.

Thin Sauce	15g butter	15g flour	300ml Milk or Stock
Pouring Sauce Medium Sauce	20g butter	20g flour	300ml Milk or Stock
Coating Sauce Thick Sauce	25g butter	25g flour	300ml Milk or Stock
Panada Very Thick Sauce	50g butter	50g flour	300ml Milk or Stock

Classic Béchamel/Velouté

**These sauces are identical at the beginning.
Béchamel will require the use of seasoned milk whilst
Velouté will use stock instead of milk.**

INGREDIENTS

20g plain flour
20g butter
300 ml milk for Béchamel 300ml well-flavoured stock for Velouté
½ small brown onion roughly diced
½ celery stick, diced
1 peeled carrot finely diced.
½ teaspoon black peppercorns
1 bouquet garni (6 sprigs parsley. 6 sprigs thyme, 1-3 small bay leaves)
Salt and white pepper to taste
A pinch of nutmeg (optional)
20 ml cream if you are making Velouté sauce.

METHOD

Place the milk in a saucepan and bring to boil with the onion, bouquet garni, carrot and celery.
Boil for 2-3 minutes and then turn the heat off and allow to cool completely.
Once cooled, strain and reserve the seasoned milk.
Measure out the butter, flour, and milk and have them ready to use.
In a medium-sized saucepan, melt the butter over medium-low heat. Be careful not to let it brown; you want it to melt and become frothy.
Once the butter is melted, add the flour. Stir constantly with a wooden spoon or a whisk to create a smooth paste, also known as a roux. Cook the roux for about 2 minutes, but do not let it brown.
Gradually pour in the seasoned milk/stock while continuing to stir. Adding the milk slowly and stirring constantly will help prevent lumps from forming.
Increase the heat to medium and continue to stir the sauce until it begins to simmer. Once it starts simmering, reduce the heat to low and let it cook through and boil through once.

IF YOU ARE MAKING Velouté - add the cream right at the end to enrich the sauce and then stir through. You can reduce the heat and let it simmer, but once it has boiled, the flour will be cooked, and you can use it. Season the sauce with salt and white pepper to taste. You can also add a pinch of nutmeg.

Daughter Sauces of Béchamel & Velouté

SAUCE ALLEMANDE AKA SAUCE PARISIENNE

INGREDIENTS

1 recipe Béchamel/Velouté sauce

2 egg yolks

40g butter

METHOD

Beat the egg yolks and the stock together, and then pour and mix into the Béchamel/Velouté sauce. Cook over extremely low heat, and cook gently, whisking ALL the time, until thickened but not split. Remove from the heat and add the butter.

This is essentially an enriched sauce and is beautifully decadent.

Use over chicken, fish or vegetables. It is so elegant.

SAUCE AURORE

INGREDIENTS

1 recipe Béchamel/Velouté sauce

2 tablespoons tomato puree

40g butter

METHOD

Whisk the tomato puree and the butter into the sauce, and then serve over your choice of chicken, eggs, pork, fish or vegetables

CAPER SAUCE

INGREDIENTS

1 recipe Béchamel/Velouté sauce

1 tablespoon chopped capers

Zest of one lemon

1 tablespoon lemon juice

1 tablespoon chopped parsley

METHOD

Simply stir in the additional ingredients and serve over fish or seafood dishes.

SAUCE CHAUDFROID

INGREDIENTS

1 recipe Béchamel/Velouté sauce

150 ml well-seasoned stock, hot

2 sheets gold strength bloomed leaf gelatine/30g gelatine powder

METHOD

Add the hot stock to the sauce and then whisk in the gelatine. Cool to a coating consistency and then use to coat boned, stuffed meat dishes.

EGG SAUCE

INGREDIENTS

1 recipe Béchamel/Velouté sauce

2 hard-boiled eggs, grated or chopped

2 tablespoons chopped parsley/dill

METHOD

Stir the chopped eggs and herbs into the sauce and serve with fish.

SAUCE A'LA' ESTRAGON/TARRAGON SAUCE

INGREDIENTS

1 recipe Béchamel/Velouté sauce

200ml white wine

4 tablespoons chopped tarragon

1 tablespoon shallot, finely chopped.

METHOD

Place the wine and half the tarragon, and the shallot in a saucepan and bring to a boil. Allow to reduce to about 2 tablespoons and then add to your sauce with the fresh tarragon.

SAUCE MORNAY

INGREDIENTS

1 recipe Béchamel/Velouté sauce

50g grated Parmesan, Cheddar or Pecorino Cheese

METHOD

While the sauce is still hot, stir in the cheese and serve. Never boil; it tends to curdle.

MUSHROOM SAUCE

INGREDIENTS

1 recipe Béchamel/Velouté sauce

100 g finely diced mushrooms of your choice

30g butter

METHOD

Place the butter in a frying pan and allow to heat. Now add the mushrooms and cook until soft and fragrant. When cooked, add the cooked mushrooms to the sauce, stir and serve.

SAUCE SOUBISE

INGREDIENTS

1 recipe Béchamel/Velouté sauce

150g diced onion

40g butter

4 tablespoons cream

METHOD

Fry the onions in the butter until soft and fragrant. Add the cream and the sauce and stir through.

SAUCE SUPREME

INGREDIENTS

1 recipe Béchamel/Velouté sauce

2 egg yolks

25g butter

40 ml cream

METHOD

Beat the eggs and cream together. While the sauce is still hot, stir in the cream, egg yolks and butter and whisk until smooth. Serve with chicken, eggs or vegetables.

Brown Sauce/Demi-Glace

INGREDIENTS

3 tablespoons oil or clarified butter
1 onion, finely chopped
1 carrot, peeled and chopped
1 stick celery, chopped
2 tablespoons flour
1 tablespoon tomato puree
300ml cold beef stock
1 bouquet Garni (parsley, bay leaf, thyme)
Freshly ground pepper
Salt to season

METHOD

Heat the butter in a medium-sized pot and add the onion, carrot, and colory and stir to cook through, about 3-4 minutes.

Once they are just about to change colour remove from the heat and then add the flour, stir it through to coat the veggies. Add the tomato puree and 2oo ml of the stock. Return to the heat and cook through for about 20 minutes. Skim the surface of the sauce frequently to remove any scum that may have risen to the top.

At this stage this sauce is referred to as sauce espagnole.

Strain this liquid to remove all the chopped vegetables. Now add the remaining stock and cook over low heat for about 20 minutes. Season to taste and use as required.

Daughter Sauces of Brown Sauce

SAUCE CHASSEUR

INGREDIENTS

1 x 300 ml batch Demi-Glace

30g butter

1 shallot, finely chopped

100g button mushrooms, finely sliced

300ml white wine

2 tablespoons tomato paste

METHOD

Melt the butter in a saucepan and cook the shallots for a few minutes, until soft and fragrant. Now add the mushrooms and wine and boil quickly until the liquid has reduced by half. Whisk the tomato puree into the sauce, season and then serve.

SAUCE DUXELLES

INGREDIENTS

1 x 300 ml batch Demi-Glace

40g butter

1 shallot, finely chopped

100g finely chopped mushrooms

150ml white wine

1 tablespoon tomato paste

3 tablespoons chopped parsley

METHOD

Melt the butter in a medium saucepan and cook the shallots and mushrooms for a few minutes until soft. Add the wine, decrease the heat and reduce this until you have about two tablespoons left over and the flavour is reduced. Now add this to your Demi-Glace, add the tomato paste, and parsley and stir through. Serve with steak, vegetables or similar.

SAUCE MADÈRE/MADEIRA SAUCE

INGREDIENTS

1 x 300 ml batch Demi-Glace

1 tablespoon tomato puree

50g sliced mushrooms

60 ml sherry

Pinch black pepper

1 tablespoon butter

METHOD

Melt the butter in a saucepan and add the mushrooms, cook for a minute or two and then add the sauce and the tomato paste and sherry. Season to taste, or reduce over a low heat. Ready to serve on steaks or other meat dishes.

House Made BBQ Sauce

SERVINGS:

INGREDIENTS

1 tablespoon canola oil
4 cloves garlic, minced
1 large onion, diced. At least a cup
1 jar 700g passata or fresh tomatoes chopped
1/3 cup molasses (you can find this at your supermarket)
1/3 cup brown sugar
4 tablespoons brown vinegar
4 tablespoons Worcestershire sauce
Pinch salt

METHOD

Heat the oil in a saucepan over medium-low heat. Add the garlic and onions and cook for 5 minutes, stirring, being careful not to burn them. Reduce the heat to low. Add the tomatoes, molasses, brown sugar and vinegar (or less to taste), Worcestershire sauce and salt and stir.

Allow to simmer for 20 minutes.

Taste after simmering and add whatever ingredient it needs (more spice, more sugar, etc.). Taste is very personal.

Sugo Sauce with Roasted Capsicum

SERVINGS: 4-6

INGREDIENTS

Olive oil to fry
1 onion finely chopped
2 cloves garlic
1/2 cup roasted red capsicums
(cut in half, place under the grill until the skin goes black, cool, and then remove skin)
700ml jar tomato passata
Salt and pepper to season
1 small chilli (optional)

METHOD

Cut the capsicums in half, deseed and then place under the grill (cut side down) until the skin is black and blistered. Allow to cool, and then peel the skin off.
Now fry the onions and the garlic in the oil until just soft.
Now add the cooked, roasted capsicum, the tomato passata/puree and the seasoning and cook through.

Simply place these gorgeous ingredients in a food processor or use a stick blender and blend until smooth. A fantastic accompaniment to a wide variety of dishes and salads and heaps of fun to garnish with.

Hot Emulsified Sauces

SAUCE BEURRE BLANC

INGREDIENTS

3 tablespoons white wine vinegar
3 tablespoons white wine
2 finely chopped shallots.
200g butter, cold, grated or finely diced
Freshly ground white pepper.

METHOD

Boil the wine vinegar, wine and shallots in a small saucepan or frying pan until reduced to about 1 tablespoon.

Reduce the heat to very, very low, and then start to whisk in the butter, one dice/spoon at a time. The butter must soften to thicken the sauce but MUST NOT MELT. This is the trick to this sauce. If the butter melts and splits, start again. Remove the pan from the heat if you need to. Do this until all the butter is incorporated and the sauce is thick and lush. Serve immediately.

You CANNOT keep this sauce hot as the butter will melt and become oily! If it is possible to keep warm in a Bain Marie.

What a wonderful skill to have! It is delicious over fish and seafood and is delightfully elegant.

SAUCE BLANCHE AU BEURRE
(WHITE SAUCE ENRICHED WITH BUTTER)

INGREDIENTS

50g butter
1 tablespoon flour
300ml boiling water/milk
White pepper to season
2 teaspoons lemon juice

METHOD

Melt 15g of the butter in a saucepan until foaming and hot. Stir in the flour QUICKLY with a whisk and then when smooth, remove from the heat. Gradually whisk in the hot, boiling water/milk, whisking constantly. Do not put this back on the heat, the flour will cook by virtue of the boiling water. Now, whisk in the remaining butter until it is incorporated. Season to taste with salt and pepper, and then add the lemon juice. Serve or use immediately.

Hollandaise Sauce

INGREDIENTS

175 butter, clarified
2 tablespoons water
3 egg yolks, beaten
A large pinch of cayenne pepper
15ml lemon juice (or to taste)

METHOD

Hollandaise is easy once you know how to handle the eggs and prevent them from curdling. If you have an unreliable heat source, you might want to find yourself a double boiler. Generally you can make one by finding existing equipment in your kitchen. To make a double boiler, fill a saucepan with about an inch of cold water. Find a metal mixing bowl that will fit over the saucepan comfortably. The mixing bowl should be wide-mouthed so you can whisk freely. Heating the eggs gently over boiling water will ensure a gentle heat in the even that your cooktop is unpredictable. Never let the base of the mixing bowl actually touch the water. When you are whisking, make sure you anticipate the steam that is present and that you have a tea towel to lift the bowl when ready. Make sure when you lift the bowl up off the steaming water, that you pull it off and then to the side to avoid a steam burn.

In a small saucepan over low heat or over a double boiler, add the eggs, water and a little salt. Add a pinch of cayenne pepper. Whisk to make a smooth paste. Set the pan over a very low heat, or start your double boiler, making sure you whisk the entire time. The eggs will only start to curdle at approximately 72-74C, so if you have a thermometer, you can monitor it like that. Whisk and cook whilst whisking until the eggs are thick and creamy and have started leaving a trail at the base of the pan. The base of the pan should NEVER GET HOT, as your eggs will curdle.

Once the eggs are thick turn the heat off and start to whisk the melted, clarified butter in slowly in a thin stream, whisking to incorporate as you go. When all the butter has been incorporated, add the lemon juice and stir through. Adjust the seasoning and serve.

Blender Hollandaise Sauce

INGREDIENTS

3 room-temperature egg yolks
2 tablespoons warm water
15 ml lemon juice
Large pinch salt
Pinch of cayenne pepper
100g butter melted and browned or clarified, warm to hot, but not boiling

METHOD

Place the egg yolks, lemon juice, warm water and seasoning in a blender and then cover with a lid. Blend on high for about 30 seconds until the eggs are smooth.

Now blend on a high speed and pour the warm, but not piping hot melted butter in a slow and steady stream through the opening in the lid. The sauce will go thick and creamy. You can then season to taste and serve.

Burnt Butter Hollandaise/Sauce Noisette

INGREDIENTS

175 butter, melted and then browned slightly until it smells nutty

2 tablespoons water

3 egg yolks, beaten

A large pinch of cayenne pepper

15ml lemon juice (or to taste)

METHOD

NOTE:

Hollandaise is easy once you know how to handle the eggs and prevent them from curdling. If you have an unreliable heat source, you might want to find yourself a double boiler. Generally you can make one by finding existing equipment in your kitchen. To make a double boiler, fill a saucepan with about an inch of cold water. Find a metal mixing bowl that will fit over the saucepan comfortably. The mixing bowl should be wide-mouthed so you can whisk freely. Heating the eggs gently over boiling water will ensure a gentle heat in the even that your cooktop is unpredictable. Never let the base of the mixing bowl actually touch the water. When you are whisking, make sure you anticipate the steam that is present and that you have a tea towel to lift the bowl when ready. Make sure when you lift the bowl up off the steaming water, that you pull it off and then to the side to avoid a steam burn. This little twist is simply delicious. You can add your choice of herbs into the butter and try different twists…it's easy and fun once you know how.

In a small saucepan over low heat or over a double boiler, add the eggs, 15ml lemon juice water and a little salt. Add a pinch of cayenne pepper. Whisk to make a smooth paste. Set the pan over a very low heat, or start your double boiler, making sure you whisk the entire time. The eggs will only start to curdle at approximately 72-74C, so if you have a thermometer, you can monitor it like that. Whisk and cook whilst whisking until the eggs are thick and creamy and have started leaving a trail at the base of the pan. The base of the pan should NEVER GET HOT, as your eggs will curdle.

Once the eggs are thick turn the heat off and start to whisk the melted, browned butter in slowly in a thin stream, whisking to incorporate as you go. Put all the bits in; they only add to the deliciousness! When all the butter has been incorporated, add any additional lemon juice to taste and stir through. Adjust the seasoning and serve.

Daughter Sauces of Hollandaise Sauce

BÉARNAISE SAUCE

INGREDIENTS

Follow the recipe for a standard Hollandaise, BUT start with this first.

3 tablespoons white wine vinegar

3 tablespoons dry white wine

4-5 peppercorns, whole

2 bay leaves

1 shallot, finely chopped

Pinch of chopped mace or use nutmeg

1 teaspoon each of freshly chopped tarragon + chervil + chives + parsley

METHOD

Start by adding the wine and the vinegar, shallots, peppercorns and bay leaves into a saucepan. Boil rapidly until the contents have reduced to about 30 ml. Remove from the heat and then strain the liquid. Follow the recipe for the hollandaise, but use your reduced wine liquid instead of the lemon juice. At the end, simply add your chopped herbs, adjust the seasoning and serve.

Béarnaise is the traditional accompaniment for chateaubriand steak.

SAUCE CHORON

INGREDIENTS

300ml batch Béarnaise Sauce

1 tablespoon tomato paste

METHOD

Simply whisk the tomato puree in and then serve immediately.

SAUCE MALTAISE

INGREDIENTS

300ml batch Béarnaise Sauce

Juice of ½ orange

1 tablespoon orange zest, julienne or zested

METHOD

Simply add the juice and zest to the Béarnaise and serve.

SAUCE MIREILLE

INGREDIENTS

300ml Hollandaise

1 tablespoon tomato puree

1 tablespoon chopped basil

METHOD

Simply stir the tomato paste and chopped basil through and serve.

SAUCE MOUTARDE

INGREDIENTS

300ml Hollandaise

1 tablespoon Dijon mustard

METHOD

Simply stir the mustard into the Hollandaise and serve

Parmesan Pepper Cream Sauce

INGREDIENTS

300 ml milk
100ml cream
20g flour mixed to a paste with 30g butter
125 g cheese Parmesan or Pecorino grated
1 pinch grated nutmeg
Salt to taste
5ml course and freshly ground pepper

METHOD

Heat the milk and cream in a heavy-based saucepan until just bubbling around the edges.
I always boil the cream and milk first to increase the flavour profile.
Now add the flour that has been mixed to a smooth paste with butter and whisk in.
Continue to stir over medium heat until the sauce thickens.

Remove from heat and season to taste with salt and freshly ground pepper.
This is then ready to be poured over the quenelle and baked. It is a very decadent and rich dish, so be sure to serve it with steamed broccolini, snow peas, etc, to give it a lift of freshness.
Place under the grill with a little extra cheese for garnish, and grill till gorgeous and hot and the sauce and cheese are bubbling.

So light and decadent. Ooh la la!

Truffled Cream Sauce

SERVINGS: 4-6

INGREDIENTS

2 tablespoons mushroom dust (food process dried mushrooms)
OR 1 cup finely minced mushroom
Half teaspoon salt OR vegetable stock powder OR stock cube
125 ml fresh cream
250 ml water
1 tablespoon truffle tapenade OR 2 tablespoons truffle oil

METHOD

Simply heat all these ingredients together over a medium heat and then allow to thicken to required consistency. Always taste before you serve, if it's too thick and salty simply add more cream or water, if it's too thin and not tasty enough, simply season with salt to taste.

Fragrant Mushroom Duxelles

SERVINGS: 4-6

INGREDIENTS

350g morel, button, assorted mushrooms, minced
1 tablespoon butter
3 tablespoons minced shallots
1 teaspoon minced thyme
100ml white wine/sherry

METHOD

First, cook off the shallots in the butter until soft and fragrant; now add the mushrooms and cook through. When dried out, add the butter and sherry/wine and cook down until reduced.

CLASSIC MAYONNAISE

Cold Emulsified Sauces

CLASSIC MAYONNAISE

INGREDIENTS

1 egg yolk at room temperature
½ teaspoon mustard
20ml lemon juice
Salt and pepper to season
150-250 ml vegetable oil

METHOD

Please do not use a cold egg...it MUST be room temperature.

Place the room-temperature egg yolk in a wide mixing bowl. Add the mustard, seasoning and lemon juice and whisk vigorously to combine.

Now pour the oil into a thin, slow stream and whisk to incorporate. You can stop at 100ml, but the more oil you add, the thicker your mayonnaise will become, so it's a personal choice, really. Season to taste.

You can then store this in the fridge for up to 2 weeks.

Porcini Black Salt Mayonnaise

INGREDIENTS

(MAKES JUST OVER 350ML)

1 egg at room temperature
3ml black salt or normal salt
15ml Dijon or grainy mustard
15 ml dried porcini, blended into a powder in a spice grinder
Pinch white pepper
15ml lemon, lime juice, white balsamic condiment or white wine vinegar
300 ml vegetable oil

METHOD

Blend these together first until nice and smooth; you can do this by hand or use a stick blender or mixer to help. Once smooth, start adding 300ml oil in a thin stream until the mixture starts to thicken; continue to pour until all the oil has been incorporated, but never add the oil too quickly or all at once.

If you curdle the mix, simply add the curdled mix using the method above, but add it into a NEW egg mixture.

Lemon Pepper Mayonnaise

MAKES JUST OVER 350ML

INGREDIENTS

1 egg at room temperature
3ml salt
5ml dijon or other mustard
Pinch black course ground pepper
Zest one lemon, then you need 15ml lemon juice
300ml sunflower/canola/rice bran oil

METHOD

Blend these together first until nice and smooth; you can do this by hand or use a stick blender or mixer to help. Once smooth start adding 300ml oil in a thin stream until the mixture starts to thicken; continue to pour until all the oil has been incorporated! If you curdle the mix, simply add the curdled mix using the method above, but add it into a NEW egg mixture.

To change the flavour and profile of your mayo, simply change the mustard to either grainy mustard or even horseradish or wasabi!
Mix and match for lots of culinary fun!

Mayonnaise Daughter Dressings

Ceasar Dressing

METHOD

Simply add 3 anchovy fillets, 1 clove garlic, 3 tablespoons parmesan, grated, to your standard Mayo

Ranch Dressing

METHOD

Simply combine:

1/3 cup each mayo, buttermilk and sour cream.

2 teaspoons each chopped dill, parsley, chives

1 garlic clove, minced

pinch black pepper

Dips & Dressings

ALL SAUCE RECIPES MAKE A SERVING SIZE OF 4-6

Beetroot, Balsamic & Rosemary Sweet Drizzling Sauce

INGREDIENTS

50-80g beetroot, very finely diced or sliced

1 teaspoon chopped rosemary

1 tablespoon balsamic vinegar/glaze

1 clove garlic crushed

Half cup white sugar

1 cup cloudy apple, pomegranate or similar juice

METHOD

Simply boil in a pan until thick and syrupy. Because of the high sugar content, you can make this in advance! It takes ABOUT 8-15 minutes

Remember! You can make your own variation of this versatile sauce simply by changing the juice and ingredients.

Tumeric Spiced Concasse

INGREDIENTS

1 kg beautifully ripe red tomatoes

100g capsicum diced or use deli fire-roasted cap

3-4 shallots finely chopped

1 teaspoon finely chopped thyme and/or oregano

3 cloves garlic, mashed

Salt and pepper to season

1 tablespoon grated turmeric

METHOD

Place a large pot of water on the stove and allow it to come to a boil. Prepare the tomatoes by making a cross in the skin at the base of the fruit. Place into boiling water and blanch. Remove and cool under running water; the skin should peel off where you have made the incision.

Quarter and then remove seeds. Chop tomato finely and set aside. Fry off the garlic, herbs, and shallots in a hot frying pan with a little oil until fragrant. Add the minced turmeric and allow to cook through before adding the tomatoes. Reduce the heat and allow the tomatoes to cook until a lovely sauce has formed..

House-made Sweet Chilli Sauce

INGREDIENTS

250 ml white sugar
2-5 chillies, chopped
Juice and zest of one lemon or lime
1 stick lemon grass, bruised & chopped
1 teaspoon ginger chopped
¼ teaspoon crushed ginger (or just one spoon of curry paste)
500 ml orange juice, fruit juice or puree, or just water
250g fruit like mango or strawberry, chopped (frozen is fine)

METHOD

Boil the ingredients together over medium heat for about ten minutes or until thick and sticky.

Remove from the heat and allow to cool before serving as a dipping sauce with spring rolls....or delicious as a salad dressing or as a sauce for chicken, beef or pork.

Basic Thai Salad Dressing

INGREDIENTS

2 tablespoons fresh lime juice
2 tablespoons fish sauce
1 teaspoon dark brown sugar
1 Thai lime leaf, finely chopped
2-3 chopped Birdseye chilis (more or less as you like)

METHOD

Whisk lime juice, fish sauce, dark brown sugar, chopped lime leaf and chilli together in a small bowl until sugar is dissolved.

Taste and adjust to your taste (spiciness, sour, sweetness).

Vietnamese Dipping Sauce

INGREDIENTS

3 tablespoons fish sauce
2 tablespoons white sugar
1/3 cup warm water
2 garlic cloves
3 red Birdseye chili
2 tablespoons lime/lemon juice

METHOD

Place chillies, garlic and sugar in a mortar and pound into a coarse paste, then transfer it into a small bowl and add the water, lime juice and fish sauce.

Stir well to dissolve.
Taste and adjust to your taste.
(spiciness, sour, sweetness) set aside.

Carrot Ginger Dressing

INGREDIENTS

1 large carrot peeled and cut roughly
1 tablespoon ginger peeled and cut roughly
1 tablespoon cider or your favourite clear vinegar
3 tablespoons peanut or veg oil
A drop of sesame oil
Pinch salt

METHOD

Blend in your smoothie maker until this forms a bright orange, velvety dressing.
Perfect on salads, over leftover vegetables or any dish at all!

Chermoula

INGREDIENTS

1 cup olive oil, please make sure it's fresh.
1 teaspoon ground cumin
1 teaspoon chilli powder
1 teaspoon salt
1 large red onion minced or finely chopped
3 cloves garlic
1 teaspoon turmeric
1 teaspoon black pepper
1 teaspoon paprika
1 teaspoon ground cinnamon
1 cup coriander leaves
1 cup parsley leaves

METHOD

THIS GORGEOUS MOROCCAN MARINADE WILL ADD ZING TO ANYTHING!
Simply whizz together in a food processor! Delicious as a drizzle over almost anything!

Chimichurri

Chimichurri

SERVINGS: 4 - 6

INGREDIENTS

1/2 cup olive oil (please make sure it's really fresh)

2 tablespoons red wine vinegar (for acidity)

1/2 cup finely chopped parsley

3-4 cloves garlic, finely chopped or minced

2 small red chillies, or 1 red chilli, deseeded and finely chopped (about 1 tablespoon finely chopped chilli)

1 teaspoon dried oregano or use 2 teaspoons fresh (my preference)

½ level teaspoon salt

½ teaspoon cracked black pepper

METHOD

Mix all ingredients together in a bowl or food processor and blend. Allow to sit for 5-10 minutes to release all of the flavours into the oil before using. Ideally, let it sit for more than 2 hours if time allows. Chimichurri can be prepared earlier than needed and refrigerated for 24 hours, if needed.

Use to baste meats (chicken or steaks) while grilling or barbecuing. Or use fresh over your choice of steaks, chicken dishes and vegetables.

Butters

Whipped Truffle or Porcini Butter

INGREDIENTS

125 g butter, grated
2 tablespoons truffle paste
OR use one fresh truffle OR use 2 tablespoons of dried porcini mushroom blended or chopped/dust.

METHOD

Place the grated butter in your stand mixer and then whip with a whisk attachment in the stand mixer bowl for approximately 15 minutes until white, whipped and light.
You will need to scrape the sides of the bowl down as you go.

Now add the truffles, truffle paste or porcini mushroom dust and whisk through.

Place in a cute bowl or spoon onto grease-proof paper, roll into a cylinder, twist the ends, and then store in the fridge or freezer.
Cut into discs when needed for bread, steak or just about anything.

Turmeric, Chilli & Lime Butter with Black Crust

INGREDIENTS

125 g butter, grated
1 teaspoon chopped chillies
1 teaspoon chopped Thai lime leaf OR use 6-8 curry leaves or 8-12 basil leaves
1/2 teaspoon fresh or ground turmeric or pinch of saffron strands
16-24 extra basil leaves to burn for the sexy black crust
1 teaspoon black peppercorns

METHOD

Place the grated butter in your stand mixer and then whip with a whisk attachment in the stand mixer bowl for approximately 15 minutes until white, whipped and light. You will need to scrape the sides of the bowl down as you go.

Now add the chillies, chopped leaves and turmeric or saffron. Take the 16-24 additional basil leaves and 'burn' and blacken them for about 6-8 minutes in your oven at 200 C or an air fryer. You want them burnt and dried. Allow the burnt leaves to cool and then food process with the black peppercorns to make a black, fragrant powder.

Sprinkle the black herb and pepper dirt onto grease-proof paper to cover the paper, spoon the whipped butter on top of this and then roll into a cylinder, making sure you have coated the outside of the butter with the black dust. Now, use a sushi mat to shape your cylinder into a square. Place in fridge or freezer to set. Cut into discs when needed for bread, steak or just about anything.

Clarified Butter

Clarified Butter

The main reason for clarifying butter is to remove the impurities and give it a higher temperature tolerance. If you have ever heated butter in a pan, it is really prone to burning very quickly.

You can clarify butter in advance and then store it in the fridge for use at a later stage.

Simply melt the butter over medium heat, and then when the white milk solids rise to the top, scoop them off and discard them on a paper towel. Continue until the butter is clear, and you only have a clear yellow butter oil left over.

Store and use at your leisure.

BURNT OR BROWN BUTTER

This is an amazing and stunningly simple way of adding elegance and flavour to a wide variety of dishes like pasta, steaks, chicken, vegetables or even bread.
You can do a simple burnt or browned butter, OR you could add ingredients to compliment the dish you are making. For instance:

Seafood and fish dishes: You could add lemon zest and dill fronts to the sauce at the beginning, and they will crisp up and flavour the butter
Steak and vegetable dishes: You could add coarsely ground black peppercorns and basil leaves for the ultimate in sophistication and taste
Various dishes: You could add various combinations of herbs like tarragon, sage, dill, chilli, and citrus rind.
Burnt/brown butters are simply delicious. I absolutely love how versatile they are…and so simple to make.

The best part is you can make them in advance and store them in the fridge for that moment when your meal just needs 'something' to lift it up.

All you need to do is melt the butter over medium to high heat in a shallow frying pan.
When the white milk solids hit the surface, stand by. Wait until the white foam boils and heats enough that the smell starts to change to a nutty caramel smell, and the colour goes from white to golden brown.
Do NOT actually burn the butter black. If it gets close and looks like it's about to burn, quickly pour the hot contents into a cold metal mixing bowl or dish.
The cold will stop the cooking process in its tracks and save your lovely sauce.

This sauce can be done really quickly, especially with a small amount of butter.
It could literally take a minute or two. The more butter you prepare, the longer it will take.
Have fun and enjoy this lovely new skill you have.

Herbed Burnt Basil & Black Pepper Butter

SERVINGS: 4-6

INGREDIENTS

100g butter grated, then beat in a stand mixer until light and pale

4 tablespoons finely chopped herbs

1 teaspoon crushed pink or black peppercorns

1 teaspoon dried edible petals (optional)

or here in this photo, I used burnt bashed basil leaves

METHOD

Simply mix together and then form into elegant herbed butter balls, you could also use a sushi mat lined with greaseproof paper to make a square block like in this picture.

You can place it in the fridge or freezer, chill and then serve with the steak.

Purées & Pastes

ALL SAUCE RECIPES MAKE A SERVING SIZE OF 4-6

Fragrant Turmeric Scented Gourmet Ceci Mash

SERVINGS: 4-6

INGREDIENTS

2 tins chickpeas drained (or use butter beans)

125 ml vegetable stock

3ml turmeric or garlic

125ml coconut cream, dairy cream to bind

3 ml stock powder or half a stock cube, or salt

METHOD

Simply heat the above ingredients together and cook until the chickpeas are slightly soft and tender.

You could add garlic and herbs to this as well.

Puree with a stick blender until super smooth, or leave as a rustic mash.

Sexy Lemon Pea Purée

SERVINGS: 4-6

INGREDIENTS

2 cups frozen peas
Half a veggie or chicken stock cube or half a teaspoon powder stock powder
80ml cream, milk or hot water
1 clove garlic crushed into a paste
Zest and juice of one lemon

METHOD

Heat the peas, stock, cream, lemon zest and garlic until the peas are JUST hot and they still have their bright green colour.

Remove from the heat and food process either in your blender or with a stick blender.
Add the lemon juice, season with salt and pepper and then blend again and serve.
Thin down with hot water to get the consistency that you want if this is too thick.

So sexy and quick and cheap and easy...my favourite things.
I use this sexy puree with fish, pork, beef or as part of a vegetable stack or goodie bowl.

Spiced Carrot Purée

SERVINGS:

INGREDIENTS

1kg carrots peeled

30ml lemon juice

Oil or olive oil

Salt and pepper, pinch ras el hanout or curry powder to season

80ml cream + some water if you need help to thin this down in the blender

METHOD

Place the seasoned, oiled carrots in a small baking dish and bake in the hot oven for half an hour until cooked and fragrant. Once slightly cooled place in a blender and add 80ml cream and blend to form a smooth paste. Add a little hot water if you need to add liquid to help thin this down.

Delicious Yellow Butterbean Purée

Delicious Yellow Butterbean Purée

SERVINGS: 4-6

INGREDIENTS

2 tins butterbeans, drained

1/2 cup cream or milk or simply increase the stock if you want to omit dairy

1 chicken/mushroom/vegetable stock cube *or use a teaspoon of stock*

2 tablespoons pecorino or parmesan grated

1 clove garlic, crushed

10 ml truffle scented oil/lemon oil or olive oil

¼ teaspoon turmeric

Salt to taste

METHOD

Place all ingredients except the oil in a large saucepan and heat over a really low heat, stirring regularly for about 10 minutes until tender, making sure that it doesn't dry out (add more cream or water/stock if needed).

Once the beans have started to break down a bit more and look more cooked, add the oil and season to taste. Either wait for these to cool and then place in a food processor, or use a hand held masher or even stick blender.

Either process completely, or leave slightly chunky for a more rustic mash!

Feel free to add some hot water to make this puree thinner if you don't want it as thick.

TO SERVE

Either serve chunky or as a puree.

NOTE

You can change the flavour of these beans to suit or match your meal. These beans can take on multiple personalities, so have fun!

* Add 1 teaspoon of chopped rosemary if you are matching lamb
* Add a teaspoon of grainy mustard or horseradish if you are matching beef or pork
* Add a teaspoon of curry powder if you are serving this with a curry
* Add smoked garlic and smoked paprika to match a Spanish theme

Chiang Mai Curry Paste

INGREDIENTS

½ teaspoon salt
4 big red chillies (or 6 long red dried chillies)
2 tablespoons fresh ginger, chopped
2 tablespoons lemon grass, chopped
6 Asian shallots or use 1 large onion
6 garlic cloves
1 tablespoon shrimp paste
1 ½ tablespoon turmeric fresh or dried

METHOD

Put all the ingredients in a mortar and pestle or in a blender until it forms a smooth, thick paste. You may need to add a little bit of water when using a blender to help the paste form

Massaman Curry Paste

INGREDIENTS

2 tablespoons each of Coriander & Cumin Seeds
6 Cardamom Pods seeds removed or use 1 ½ teaspoon ground
1 teaspoon of ground cinnamon or 1 piece of bark
6 cloves (whole)
½ teaspoon salt
1 small red onion or 9 shallots
6 cloves garlic
2 lemongrass stalks chopped
2 tablespoons grated ginger
6 long red dried chillies or use fresh

METHOD

Start by dry roasting the spices if they are not already roasted. Place in a hot oven of 200c for 3-8 minutes until fragrant or dry roast in a pan. Allow to cool and then bash to a paste in the pestle and mortar; once the spices are ground, add the 'wet' ingredients and bash to form a smooth paste. Done. Store or use straight away. Delicious.

Desserts

"I think every woman should have a blowtorch" - Julia Child

Beautiful Blueberry Pancakes (Keto or Traditional)

SERVINGS: 2-4

INGREDIENTS

BERRY PANCAKES

1 cup berries, diced if strawberry or just use whole for any other
200g plain flour
1 teaspoon baking powder
1 egg
300ml buttermilk or milk
50g melted butter
pinch of salt
5ml vanilla extract
2 teaspoons sugar (optional)
Vegetable oil or butter to cook
Syrup, cream or your favourite topping!

KETO VERSION

1 cup berries, diced if strawberry or just use whole for any other
200g almond meal
60g coconut flour or similar
1 teaspoon gluten-free baking powder
4 eggs
100ml cream
250ml water
50g melted butter or coconut oil
pinch of salt
5ml vanilla extract
2 teaspoons sweetener of your choice
Vegetable oil or butter to cook
Syrup, cream or your favourite topping!

METHOD

Simply place all these ingredients together and stir, there is no need to complicate!

If you are using a NutriBullet or Food Processor, omit the berries and then stir them in once you have the batter. Or else they will puree…

Heat and grease a frying pan over a medium heat. Once nice and hot, pour some of the batter into the pan.

Once a nice brown crust has formed, use a suitable-sized egg lift to flip these over.

Do the other side and then remove it onto a plate.

Stack and serve!

CHEF'S NOTE

For the KETO recipe, I decided to get you to make a bigger batch so you can have some leftover batter for a few days time. You can make this batter the day before your next beach BBQ or picnic; take it along and cook it on the spot!

Crepe Citronelle a 'la Chef Mel

SERVINGS: 4-6

INGREDIENTS

CREPE
1 cup plain flour
2 eggs
2 cups milk
3 tablespoons vegetable oil or melted butter
Pinch of salt

SAUCE (per person)
3 tablespoons butter
3 tablespoons sugar
Juice and zest of two oranges
Juice and zest of half a lemon
30ml brandy to flame

METHOD

Make the crepes by mixing the ingredients together in no particular order to create a thin, lump-free batter. Chill in the fridge until ready to use.
When ready, grease a non-stick pan and pour some of the batter into the pan,
cook lightly on each side and fold into triangles as per demo. Chill until ready, or use straight away.

SAUCE
Place the butter and the sugar in a pan and stir over medium heat until the butter has melted, the sugar has melted, and the mixture is bubbling. Continue to cook until the mixture caramelises, you will know when this is happening by first of all the lovely brown colour, and also the amazing delicious smell! That is why I LOVE this dessert.

Now add the juice and zest and reduce the heat, allow to cook through for about 2-5 minutes and then add as many crepes as you need. Allow them to heat through. Then, increase the heat again. When bubbling viciously, add the brandy and flambé.
Serve with ice cream!

Cannoli

SERVINGS: 6-8

INGREDIENTS

SHELLS

1 cup plain flour

1 tablespoon sugar

half an egg

1 tablespoon milk

30ml red or white wine

1 tablespoon vegetable oil

*Use the other half of the egg to seal the edges,
generally, you can water this down to make it easier and thinner to paint.*

FILLING

2 cups smooth ricotta

5 ml vanilla paste

zest of one lemon

1/4 cup icing mixture, sifted

nuts or crushed chocolate or chocolate curls to decorate

METHOD

To make the shell dough simply place all the ingredients together and mix together with a strong spoon until it comes together like a messy dough ball. Place on a floured surface, flour your hands and then knead to form a smooth, silky dough. It should take about three to five minutes of good, strong kneading.

Rest the dough for 5-10 minutes and then divide into two pieces. Roll each piece out, trying to keep it as a nice neat rectangle; you can either roll on your floured surface or use a pasta roller to get it nice and thin.

Once the sheets have all been rolled and they are nice and thin, use a large circular cutter to make about 10cm rounds.

Have your vegetable oil ready to start frying; it must be hot enough to bubble as the dough hits, but not so hot that it burns! Place the dough over the cannoli mould, seal with a little of the egg as per the demo and then seal, press and fry. You will have to hold down the cannoli to make sure all the dough is cooked. Remove from oil when lovely and golden, not too dark, and then drain on a paper towel and allow to cool.

Once cool, mix all the filling ingredients together and place in a piping bag, pipe into cooled shells and then dip the ends in either crushed chocolate, chocolate curls, roasted almond nibs or pistachio roasted! Enjoy!

Pastry Cream - Crème Patissiere

SERVINGS: 6-8

INGREDIENTS

500ml milk
100g sugar
5ml Vanilla extract or paste
4 egg yolks
70g flour

METHOD

Start by bringing the milk to a boil. This not only changes the flavour of your pastry cream but will also aid in speeding up the entire process.

Beat the eggs and sugar together until light and fluffy, and the sugar has dissolved. Add the flour and vanilla and mix to a smooth paste. Now add the boiled milk gradually and stir to combine. Place back in the pot and cook until nice and thick, about a minute.
Sprinkle with a little sugar to prevent skin from forming, OR use a sheet of plastic film.
Allow to come to room temperature and then chill in the fridge. Pop in a piping bag or use as desired.

May be stored in the fridge for up to seven days! Imagine the marvellous creations we can make!

Delicous Versatile Nougat

SERVINGS: 6-8

INGREDIENTS

4 tablespoons icing mixture to coat a greased baking sheet to set these
200g toasted almonds/pistachio/hazelnuts or combination of those
560g (2 1/2 cups) sugar
80ml (1/3 cup) water
500g glucose syrup
4 egg whites, at room temperature
1 teaspoon vanilla essence
1 teaspoon fresh or dried petals (optional)

METHOD

Place the sugar, glucose syrup and water in a medium saucepan and place over high heat. Stir with a wooden spoon, brushing down the sides of the pan occasionally with a pastry brush dipped in warm water, until the sugar dissolves, this should take about 10 minutes but will depend on your stove top!

Fill a sink with 10cm of cold water. Place the egg whites in a large stand mixer bowl. When the syrup reaches about 100°C start to whisk the egg whites until firm peaks form, add the vanilla extract. You must use a stand mixer for this as you'll need a strong motor!

When the sugar syrup reaches 150°C, immediately remove the pan from heat and place the base of the pan in the sink of cold water for 5 seconds, or until the bubbles subside. With the beater on highest speed, slowly pour hot syrup into the egg whites in a thin, steady stream. Try not to pour the syrup down side of the bowl or onto the whisk as it may set before being incorporated into egg whites.

Now whisk for a further 2-3 minutes or until the mixture is thick and glossy. Use a wooden spoon to mix the almonds and flower petals into egg white mixture until well combined. It is important to work quickly or the nougat will begin to set. Also make sure the nuts and any other fillings are at room temperature or the mixture will set too rapidly.

Spoon the nougat into a greased and icing sugar dusted baking sheet with a wet spoon to help smooth it in. Allow to set and enjoy!

Pistachio Lemon Butter Cookies

SERVINGS: 6-8

INGREDIENTS

1 cup or 225g butter
1 cup or 220g white sugar
(Cream these ingredients together in the stand mixer with the whisk attachment)

NOW ADD
1 teaspoon vanilla
Zest of one small lemon
1 egg
3 cups or 450 g plain flour
1 teaspoon baking powder
3 tablespoons finely chopped pistachio, or use the nut you prefer
half a teaspoon salt

METHOD

Mix into the whipped butter and sugar mix until it just forms a lovely firm dough. Cover with a wet cloth and allow to rest in the fridge for about 15 minutes. We are now ready to roll these out to about 5-8mm and use your fabulous cookie cutters to get the shape you want.

Place on a greased baking sheet and bake at 180 for about 12-18 minutes, until the cookies are brown and delicious and then allow to cool.

Vanilla Apple Lattice Pie (Jalousie)

SERVINGS: 6-8

INGREDIENTS

PIE	ICING
2 sheets of puff pastry	1 cup icing sugar mixed to a paste with
2 large apples cored and then sliced	Hot water (to bind, about a tablespoon) but you
(can also use pears, mangos, nectarines and peaches)	will need to adjust until it is the right thickness)
3 tablespoons apricot jam	1 teaspoon vanilla extract or essence
50 ml milk to brush pastry	
250 ml really thick custard blended with 100 ml cream	
2 tablespoons white sugar to dredge over pastry	

METHOD

Cut the pastry in half lengthways.

Place the apricot jam onto one half of the pastry, taking care to leave a border of about 2 cm.

Dollop the cup of thick custard on top of the apricot jam, and take care to leave the border clean.

Place the sliced apples neatly on top of the jam.

Fold the remaining piece of pastry in half lengthways and slice on the fold to create a lattice, taking care to leave a border of about 2 cm.

Brush the filled pastry on the border with the milk and then top with the second piece of pastry.

Brush again with the milk and then dredge with sugar.

Bake in a preheated oven of 200c for about 15 – 20 minutes until golden.

Remove from heat and then drizzle with the glaze icing.

Reserve a little of the glaze icing and mix with a teaspoon of cocoa powder, mix until smooth.

Drizzle over the white glaze as a delectable contrast.

Serve hot or cold with ice cream or cream… deliciously simple.

It will slice into at least 8 slices, but you can make them smaller.

Easy Crumble

SERVINGS: 8-12

INGREDIENTS

1 cup plain flour
½ cup butter diced
1/3 cup white sugar
1 teaspoon vanilla

METHOD

Place all these ingredients into a food processor and blend until it forms crumbs.
This can be used over cooked fruit of your choice, dulce leche, custard and more.
Be creative, so versatile and can be made in advance, frozen for up to 3 months, and used from frozen.
Bake for approximately 15 minutes in an oven of 190 c until brown and delicious.
The cooking time will depend on what filling you have placed your crumbs on.

Champagne & Rose Water Jellies Scented with Orange Zest

SERVINGS: 6-8

INGREDIENTS

250ml champagne/wine/juice of your choice

Zest and juice of one orange

30ml rose cordial

Petals, etc., to decorate

2 sheets gelatine

METHOD

Heat the champagne, zest, juice and cordial together until just about to simmer. Soak the gelatin in cold water until it just starts to soften, drain in your hand and then stir into the hot liquid. Pour into your container and allow it to set.

Decorate with fresh petals if you wish.

Brulé with Famous Tappy Tap Sugar

SERVINGS: 4-6

INGREDIENTS

300ml cream, scalded (bring to the boil just once) with:
1 vanilla pod, seeds scraped or 1 teaspoon vanilla paste/extract
60g sugar
4 large egg yolks

METHOD

Bring the cream, sugar and vanilla to the boil and then remove from the heat.
Now add hot cream in a thin stream to the beaten egg yolks (from a distance- like a long-distance relationship) and mix until smooth.
Strain through a sieve to make sure your mixture is perfectly silky, and then pour into your ramekin or baking dishes.
Bake in a bain-marie in an oven of 160-170c for about 25- 45 minutes until the custards are nicely set.
THE COOKING TIME WILL DEPEND ON YOUR RAMEKIN SIZE, SO PLEASE ADJUST THE COOKING TIME IF NECESSARY. To test if they are set, give them a little shake, or tap on the side with a spoon...there should be no ripple in the middle. If there is a ripple, you can bake for a further five minutes and test again. They will set a little bit more when they are cold.
Remove from oven and cool to room temperature. Now chill completely in the fridge.
When cool, add about 1 teaspoon of sugar to the top of the custard. You should have a 'window pane' of sugar coating the custard. Now, use your blowtorch to make the caramelised sugar!

You could make these up to three days in advance, but you would only caramelise the sugar just before serving.

Baked Sweet Soufflés

Baked Sweet Soufflés

SERVINGS: 4-6

INGREDIENTS

160ml milk
160ml cream
50g sugar (plus extra sugar for dusting ramekins)
20g flour
20 g cornflour
50g butter (plus extra butter for greasing ramekins)
4 eggs, separated

FLAVOURS

Choose **one** of the following:

100g chocolate chips + 2 teaspoons orange zest OR
200ml passionfruit pulp thickened over heat with 20g cornflour (cook once, then cool)
100g lemon curd
30 ml vanilla paste

METHOD

Heat the milk and cream in a saucepan with the sugar, and boil through once. Remove from the heat. Place your egg yolks into a bowl and beat.
Mix the 50g butter and the flours together into a paste (beurre manie), and then whisk this paste into the hot milk and cream, whisking to make sure it mixes in easily.

Cook this through once, stirring all the time, to form a thick sauce.
Now add the flavour of your choice from above; if it is the chocolate option, the sauce is still hot enough to melt the chocolate. Remove from the heat and whisk to cool slightly. Now, slowly add the beaten egg yolks; please make sure your sauce is not too hot, as the yolks will curdle. Once the sauce is smooth, set aside. Now beat the egg whites until they form stiff peaks.
Fold the egg whites into your sauce, taking care NOT to overfold. Rather leave visual egg whites than stir completely. Your mission is to keep as much of the aerated egg white as this is where your soufflé will get its best lift. Be gently handling these; no bashing or tapping!

Grease your ramekins with a pastry brush and some butter, 'painting' upwards up the side of the dish. Lightly dust the greased ramekins with sugar, then shake out the excess sugar. Fill the ramekins and then smooth the tops with a palette knife; you can run your finger around the edges to make a top hat shape. Now bake in an oven of 190 C for approximately 12-15 minutes until the mixture is no longer glossy but is matt and risen. Remove from the oven and serve!

Cold Lemon or Passionfruit Soufflé

SERVINGS: 4-6

INGREDIENTS

These are set using gelatine and are not baked
3 eggs separated
225 g sugar
1 tablespoon gelatine powder melted in 1 tablespoon warm water
or 2 sheets gold strength gelatine leaves, bloomed
300ml cream
5 ml vanilla paste or extract
100ml fresh lemon juice/orange juice/passionfruit pulp

METHOD

You can make this in individual ramekin dishes.
To prepare the ramekins, tie a collar of greaseproof paper around each ramekin with string to allow for extra height for your soufflé over the rim of the ramekin. Make the height about 5-8 cm above the ramekin.

Now, beat the cream and the vanilla until it forms stiff peaks. Separate the eggs and place the yolks into a heat-proof glass or metal bowl with the sugar; place the bowl over a pot with about 2 cm of water, the water should not touch the bottom of the bowl (double boiler) and then whisk the egg and sugar over the heat until it gets pale and thick.
Remove from the heat and then stir in your dissolved powder OR bloomed leaf gelatine. Make sure it all dissolves and the mixture is smooth. Allow to cool.
Whip the egg whites until stiff peaks have formed, and then fold the cream and the stiff egg whites into this mixture, taking care not to overheat.
Now spoon this mixture into the collared ramekins and smooth the tops with a palette knife. Place in the fridge and allow to set for about 6-8 hours. You can then 'peel' off the collars and serve your soufflé. Here i have piped meringue as a decoration.

Pear & Ricotta Tarts

SERVINGS: 6-8

INGREDIENTS

TART SHELL
- 1 ½ cups / 180g plain flour
- 60g almond meal, toasted
- ½ cup / 110g sugar
- 140g cold butter, chopped
- Zest of 1 Orange

FILLING
- 500g ricotta
- 100ml cream
- 80g sugar
- 1 teaspoon vanilla paste
- Zest of 1 orange
- 4 egg yolks
- 1-2 pears, sliced thin

METHOD

Place all tart shell ingredients in a food processor and combine until the mixture comes together. Cover with cling film and refrigerate for 30 minutes.

Press pastry into tart cases and trim. Bake in a moderate oven (170°C) for 10 minutes until just slightly browned. Remove from oven and allow to cool.

FILLING

Simply mix the ricotta and the cream together until smooth; now add the vanilla, sugar, yolks, and zest and mix until smooth and well combined. Once the tart shells are cooked and cooled, you can spoon them in and then top them with sliced pear. Bake again for about 8-12 minutes until the ricotta is set, and then cool and serve.

CHEF'S NOTE:

You can use a large tart case with this recipe. Your cooking times will vary.

Catalan Custard Tarts

Catalan Custard Tarts

SERVINGS: 6-8

INGREDIENTS

TART SHELL
1 ½ cups / 180g plain flour
60g almond meal, toasted
½ cup / 110g sugar
140g cold butter, chopped
Zest of 1 Orange

FILLING
250ml milk
200ml cream
50g sugar
1 teaspoon vanilla paste
Zest of 1 orange
Cinnamon stick
2 tablespoons butter
2 tablespoons flour

METHOD

TART SHELL

Place all ingredients in a food processor and combine until the mixture comes together. Cover with cling film and refrigerate for 30 minutes. Press pastry into tart cases and trim. Bake in a moderate oven (170°C) for 10 minutes until just slightly browned. Remove from oven and allow to cool.

FILLING

Bring the milk, cream, sugar, vanilla and orange zest to the boil in a saucepan.
Allow to cool slightly.
Combine butter and flour together to make a paste.
Using a whisk, stir the butter and flour paste into the milk mixture over low heat until the mixture thickens. This is to cook the flour through. Spoon mixture into cooked pastry cases. Dust with cinnamon and refrigerate until ready to serve.

NOTE:

You can use a large tart case with this recipe. Your cooking times will vary.

Lime & Palm Sugar Creams with Famous Tappy Tap Sugar

SERVINGS: 4-6

INGREDIENTS

400ml coconut cream
1 teaspoon lime zest
60g palm sugar grated
4 large egg yolks
Berries, mint or mango to decorate.

METHOD

Bring the cream, zest, and palm sugar to a boil and then remove them from the heat. Allow cooling.

Add the coconut cream mixture to the beaten egg yolks and mix until smooth.
Strain through a sieve to make sure your mixture is perfectly silky, and then pour into your ramekin or baking dishes. Bake in a bain-marie in an oven of 160-170°C for about 25 minutes until the custards are nicely set.
THE COOKING TIME WILL DEPEND ON YOUR RAMEKIN SIZE, SO PLEASE ADJUST THE COOKING TIME IF NECESSARY.
Remove from oven and cool before adding 1 teaspoon WHITE sugar to the top of the custard and use a blowtorch to make the caramelised sugar!

You could make these up to three days in advance, but you would only caramelise the sugar just before serving.

Sexy Honeycomb for Dessert Bling

SERVINGS: 6-12

INGREDIENTS

1.5 cups sugar
½ cup honey
80ml water
2 tablespoons golden syrup
2 teaspoons of sieved bicarbonate of soda

METHOD

NOTE

Cook to a lighter honeycomb colour rather than dark as the mixture will continue cooking when you remove from heat and add the bicarb-move quickly.

Combine the honey, sugar, water and syrup in a saucepan. Place over low heat, brushing any sugar down off the sides with a wet brush until the syrup reaches 154c or crack stage on a sugar thermometer or place in a glass of water when it forms toffee, it is ready.

Remove from heat and then immediately add in the bi-carb with a sieve and then use a strong whisk to whisk through, making sure to mix the bi-carb thoroughly through the mixture. Be careful! Let this bubble up. Do not over-stir, as you will damage the valuable bubbles created by the bicarb.

Have a stainless steel bowl at the side in case you need to remove the honeycomb from the pan if it continues to cook too much, and then carefully pour it onto greased baking paper straight on a bench or a heatproof tray. Allow to set on the bench! Have a spare stainless steel bowl on the side in case when the bicarb is added the heat of the pan burns the honeycomb.
One can make long shards to decorate with!
*This mixture can be frozen in glad bags for another day.

Spun Sugar

SERVINGS: 6-8

INGREDIENTS

1 cup sugar
1/2 cup water

METHOD

Simply dissolve 1 cup sugar and half a cup of water together in a frying pan. Shake the pan until the sugar has dissolved in the water. You can use a pastry brush and additional water to brush any sugar that may remain on the side of the pan.

Boil hot and fast until the sugar starts to go brown and goes caramel colour. This will take about 8-12 minutes, but stay close as it depends on your stovetop. Now, use two forks and dip the back of the forks into the hot caramel. Touch the two forks with the tacky caramel and pull them apart as wide as your arms will go. This will pull the sugar into thin strands, and it will set to hard in this lovely long strand. Break off carefully and keep to the side. Repeat until you have lots of strands, and then you can shape it. You can also spin the sugar over various shapes as long as they are heat-proof. if you don't want to spin the sugar, simply pour it onto a greased baking tray or ceramic tile and allow it to set. You can then bash it up into sugar gravel.

Blood Orange & Lemon Curd

SERVINGS: 4-6

INGREDIENTS

½ cup blood orange juice
½ cup lemon juice
200g salted butter
¾ cup white sugar
4 egg yolks

METHOD

Place the juices, butter and sugar in a saucepan and bring to a boil over medium heat. Remove from the heat and then add the hot mixture into the the lightly beaten yolks, using a thin steam from a long distance to cool the mixture as you add it.

Strain through a fine sieve. Add back to the saucepan.
Mix well and then use a whisk, and stir constantly over low heat for about 2-3 minutes or until the mixture has thickened. Allow to cool.

Ice Cream, Gelato, Semi Freddo, Sorbet & Panna Cotta

Bruleè scented Ice Cream with Nutted Caramel Shards

Bruleè scented Ice Cream with Nutted Caramel Shards

SERVINGS: 6-8

INGREDIENTS

800 ml fresh cream and one seeded vanilla pod, scalded and then cooled
4 eggs yolks beaten until thick and fluffy with 100g castor sugar
1 teaspoon vanilla paste

NUTTED CARAMEL
1/2 cup pecan nuts
1/2 cup white sugar
4 tablespoons hot water
2 ml flake salt
pinch of cinnamon or nutmeg

METHOD

Once the cream and the vanilla pod have come to a boil, take off the heat and allow to cool immediately.
Once slightly cooled, beat in the whipped egg yolks and sugar.
Stir over a gentle heat until the 'custard' coats the back of a spoon and has thickened.
Never go above 80C here, as it will curdle.
Cool in the fridge or freezer and then churn in the ice cream machine for about 20 minutes or until it looks like a soft serve. Place into a container that can go into the freezer, and then freeze until firm.

NUTTED CARAMEL
Place the sugar and the water in a frying pan and add the salt.
Bring to the boil, shaking while it starts to boil, making sure that all the sugar gets dissolved.
Boil the sugar syrup until it starts to go light brown caramel, and starts to smell like caramel too.

Remove from the heat, add the nuts and spices and shake to coat the nuts.
Pour the caramel-coated nuts onto a greased metal tray and allow to cool. Serve with the ice cream.

Gelato - you choose your flavour!

SERVINGS: 8-12

INGREDIENTS

5ml vanilla bean paste
(You can add 100g chocolate chips to the hot liquid, OR you can add your choice of fruit puree, and spices into the cold liquid BEFORE it boils)
600ml cream
600ml full cream milk
6 egg yolks
100g sugar

METHOD

Boil the cream and milk with the vanilla, taking care to stir while it comes to a boil. Once boiled, remove from heat and allow to cool slightly. Adding lavender or cinnamon to the cold milk at the beginning means that the flavours will infuse by the time the milk and cream have boiled.

Whisk the egg yolks and sugar in a mixer with the whisk attachment (or by hand whisk) until pale, light, and fluffy. Now, pour the boiled cream and milk into the egg mixture. If the liquid is still very hot, pour from a distance or add a bit of the hot liquid to the eggs, stirring all the time, to temper the eggs.
Once combined, strain into a heat-proof bowl. Place the bowl over a double boiler and then stir until the mixture becomes warm; take care not to let this boil, or it will be a disaster.

Once the 'custard' heats and thickens, and you can draw a line on the back of the spoon without it bleeding back, remove it from the heat. Allow to cool, chill the mixture down in the fridge or even freezer, and then churn in an ice cream machine OR place in a suitable freezer dish and whisk up with a beater every 30 or so minutes to ensure this stays creamy.

Once set and creamy, you can freeze until required.

Burnt Pear Butter Gelato

SERVINGS: 6-8

INGREDIENTS

5ml vanilla bean paste
550ml cream and 550ml full cream milk
6 egg yolks
100g dark brown sugar
2 pears cored and diced
80 g butter
40g sugar
Pinch of flake salt

METHOD

Place pear, butter, 40g sugar and salt and heat until sugar and butter have dissolved and start to caramelize and smell like heaven. Cool.

Boil the cream and milk with the vanilla and the lavender OR cinnamon taking care to stir while it comes to the boil. Once boiled remove from heat and allow to cool slightly, add the sugar and stir to dissolve. Whisk the eggs yolks until just nice and loose. Now pour in the boiled cream and milk and sugar into the egg mixture. If the liquid is still very hot pour from a distance or add a bit of the hot liquid to the eggs, stirring all the time, to temper the eggs. Once combined strain into a heat-proof bowl. Add the pear caramel. Place the bowl over a double boiler and then stir until the mixture becomes warm, take care not to let this boil or it will be a disaster!

Once the 'custard' heats and thickens, and you can draw a line on the back of the spoon without it bleeding back, remove from the heat. Allow to cool, chill the mixture down in fridge or even freezer, and then churn in an ice cream machine OR place in suitable freezer dish and whisk up with beater every 30 or so minutes to ensure this stays creamy.
Once set and creamy you can freeze until required!

Vanilla Ice Cream with Salted Pistachio Toffee

SERVINGS: 6-8

INGREDIENTS

ICE CREAM

600ml thickened cream
1 tin condensed milk
10ml vanilla extract

TOFFEE

1 cup white sugar
1/4 cup water
2 tablespoons pistachio
1/2 teaspoon black or white flake salt

METHOD

Beat the cream and vanilla until stiff peaks form. Fold in the condensed milk using a metal spoon or plastic spatula. Place in a container with a lid and place in the freezer.

TOFFEE

Place the sugar and water in a large frying pan and boil over high heat.
Shake to dissolve the sugar and allow to cook until the sugar syrup goes brown.

When brown and caramel, pour onto a greased baking sheet and top with the pistachios.
Break into small pieces when cold, and then sprinkle on top of the ice cream before it sets.

Lime & Coconut Ice Cream

SERVINGS: 6-8

INGREDIENTS

COCONUT ICE CREAM
1 litre of coconut CREAM
(don't use coconut milk as the fat content is too low)
Juice of two limes
2 kaffir limes finely chopped to make dust
100g palm sugar grated
1 tin condensed milk

LIME SYRUP
100ml sugar
250 ml water
2 lime leaves finely shredded or chopped

METHOD

Mix the ingredients together and stir to dissolve the grated palm sugar.

Place in a freezer-proof container and freeze until firm. Take a whisk or an electric beater, and then churn and mix up the ice cream to cream up any crystals. Freeze and again and repeat in a few hours…we want this to be super smooth!

SERVE AS IS OR WITH THIS LIME SYRUP AND PUREE OF STRAWBERRY

Simply boil this sugar syrup for about 20 minutes over medium heat until the sugar has dissolved and formed a thin, sticky syrup.
Simply puree 1 cup of strawberries into a lovely thick pulp.
Serve with the ice cream! So fresh and delicious!

Bruleé Scented Semi Freddo with Tappy Tap Sugar

SERVINGS: 6-8

INGREDIENTS

600 ml fresh cream, whipped
4 eggs, room temp
1 teaspoon vanilla paste
100 g castor sugar

METHOD

Simply beat the eggs, vanilla, and sugar until nice and fluffy, and then fold into the whipped cream. Place into a container that can go into the freezer, and then freeze until firm.

Serve with fresh berries and flower petals, it is gorgeous and SO versatile.
You could add melted chocolate or even cream cheese to this to change the flavours. My sons used to call caramelised sugar tappy tap sugar, so that's why I named this recipe that.

For the tappy tap sugar, place 1 teaspoon of white sugar on top of the frozen ice cream and use a blow torch to caramelise the top of the dessert.

Please get yourself a decent blowtorch, I recommend a plumbers torch that has a butane gas canister, not the ones that need to be refilled constantly.

House-Made Ice Cream Cone or Basket

SERVINGS: 8-12

INGREDIENTS

2 eggs
½ cup white sugar
¼ cup melted and cooled butter
3 tablespoons milk
1 teaspoon vanilla bean paste or extract
1/3 cup plain flour
pinch salt
Canola cooking spray to grease the pan

METHOD

Simply mix all the ingredients together to form a smooth batter. Pour into a squeezy bottle OR just leave in the container you've mixed this in and chill for about 20 minutes in the fridge.

Now heat a frying pan and spray with canola cooking spray (do not use olive oil spray.
It will make everything stick)
Make crisscross shapes in the pan to make/weave a 'net'.
Keep the lines nice and thin and crisscross to make the net strong.
When the first side has browned, use an egg lifter to turn it over. Just lightly brown the second side and then remove it from the pan and drape it over the back of a bowl so that it sets in a bowl shape.
These can be made in advance or to order!

Spiced Milk 'sorbet'

SERVINGS: 4-6

INGREDIENTS

1 cup white sugar
1 cup hot water
10 ml vanilla bean paste
1 teaspoon cinnamon or chai spice
3 cups full cream milk

METHOD

Boil the milk and spice either in the microwave or in a pot on the stove, and set aside to cool.

Boil the sugar and the water together for about 8 minutes on a nice hot cooktop until a thick but still white syrup has formed. Stir into the milk and vanilla and then cool, chill in the freezer and then add to an ice cream churn and churn until smooth.

So delicious as a simple sorbet. Sorbet does not usually have dairy, but this one does.

Lime & Coconut Panna Cotta

SERVINGS: 4-6

INGREDIENTS

400ml coconut cream
100ml coconut milk
juice and zest of one lime
3 tablespoons Thai basil
80g palm sugar
2 sheets leaves gold strength gelatine

METHOD

Bring the cream, milk, Thai basil, lime zest, and sugar to a boil. Remove from heat and allow to cool slightly. Soak the gelatine in cold water for a few minutes until very soft. Now stir into the warm milk and cream.

Strain to remove basil and zest, and then pour into the following:

Lightly oil 6 x ½ cup moulds or ramekins OR pour into cute glass jars or tea cups.

Strain the cream mixture (to remove the herbs and give a silky smooth result) and pour it into the ramekins. Refrigerate until ready to serve.

TO SERVE

Break the seal of the panna cotta by using a small knife to run around the edge of the mould. Turn onto a serving plate and shake to release. Serve with your choice of fresh fruit, biscuit, dessert dust or sugar shards and bling with fresh petals.

Vanilla Panna Cotta

Vanilla Panna Cotta

SERVINGS: 4-6

INGREDIENTS

400ml cream
100ml milk
60g white sugar or use honey, maple or sweetener
2 sheets gold strength leaf gelatine
5 ml vanilla paste or extract.

METHOD

Heat the cream, milk, vanilla, and sugar to a boil. Remove from heat and allow to cool slightly.
Soak the gelatine in cold water for no more than 1 minute. Remove from water and squeeze. Now stir into the warm milk and cream. Pour the cream mixture into greased dariole moulds or ungreased glass jars, allow it to come to room temperature, and refrigerate until ready to serve. Best chilled for 6 hours or overnight to allow the gelatine to set.

TO SERVE

Break the seal of the panna cotta by using a small knife to run around the edge of the mould. Turn onto a serving plate and shake to release.
Serve with your choice of fresh fruit, biscotti, dessert dust or sugar shards and bling with fresh petals. In this photo, I used Persian floss.

CHEF'S NOTE

Panna Cotta is so versatile. You can change the flavour as many times as you like.
Try these variations for years of panna cotta fun!

COFFEE PANNA COTTA:
Omit 100 ml of the cream and replace it with 100 ml of strong coffee instead.

CHOCOLATE PANNA COTTA:
Add 50g melted chocolate and 1 tablespoon cocoa to the recipe, no need to adjust the liquids here as the chocolate will set beautifully.

LEMON MERINGUE PANNA COTTA:
Omit 50ml of cream and add 50ml strained lemon juice AFTER you have boiled the cream and milk in the standard recipe, you will only add the lemon juice after you have boiled the mixture.
Then add the lemon juice and the bloomed gelatine. you can also pipe the panna cotta once it has set with meringue and blow torch it to make a lemon meringue panna cotta...it's the BEST.

BERRY PANNA COTTA:
Omit 100 ml of the cream in the recipe and replace it with 100ml strained berry puree of your choice, then follow the recipe as normal.

BOOZY PANNA COTTA:
Omit 50-100 ml of the cream in the standard recipe and then replace it with whisky, rum, or creamy liquor of your choice and then follow the standard method and recipe.

Chocolate

Gourmet Chocolate Tarts

Gourmet Chocolate Tarts

SERVINGS: 6-8

INGREDIENTS

TART SHELL

1 ½ cups / 180g plain flour
60g Dutch cocoa for a chocolate base
OR almond meal for a white base (toast the almond meal if using)
½ cup / 110g sugar
140g cold butter, chopped

FILLING

2 eggs
2 egg yolks
¼ cup / 55g sugar
1 teaspoon vanilla extract
250g dark chocolate
200g butter

METHOD

TART SHELL

In a food process place flour, cocoa or almond meal and sugar and butter until the mixture resembles fine breadcrumbs. Add egg and then process just until the ingredients come together.
Wrap and refrigerate for at least 30 minutes and then press into your prepared 24cm round tin OR I often use my smaller silicone or loose-base shells for individual tarts.
Press the crumbly pastry into the tart shell, pressing with your fingers OR a flat bottom of a dish like a ramekin dish, to compact the crumbs and create a pastry. Trim the excess with a sharp paring knife, and then prick bases all over with a fork.
Bake for 10 minutes or until just slightly brown. Bake at about 170c. Remove from heat and allow to cool.

FILLING

Melt the chocolate and the butter together either over a double boiler or in the microwave.
Now whisk eggs, egg yolks and sugar in a beater with the whisk until light and fluffy. Add the delicious chocolate butter mix and then stir to combine.
Place mixture into cooked tart shells and then bake at 180 for about 5 minutes until just the cap of the filling is set. Remove from over and allow to cool to room temp and then refrigerate until cold.
Serve dusted with cocoa powder.

Death by Chocolate Marshamallow Ice Cream using Paté a Bombe

SERVINGS: 8-12

INGREDIENTS

6 egg yolks
50ml water in a pan with 170g sugar
5ml vanilla paste
100g melted chocolate

METHOD

Heat the water and sugar until making sure you have a temperature probe ready!
Whisk up the egg yolks for about 5-7 minutes until light and fluffy.
When the sugar hits 120 C, then remove it from the heat.
Pour into the eggs with the beater on LOW and add slowly until incorporated.
Mix for a further minute to combine, add the melted chocolate and vanilla, whisk until cool and then refrigerate or freeze.

Death by Chocolate Platter featuring 'Spiced' Death by Chocolate Brownies

Death by Chocolate Platter featuring 'Spiced' Death by Chocolate Brownies

SERVINGS: 8-12

INGREDIENTS

250 g unsalted butter
200g dark chocolate
4 large eggs
360g castor sugar
65g plain flour
1tsp baking powder
5ml sweet Ras el Hanout
80g cocoa powder
100g chocolate chips/ roasted nuts

CHOCOLATE TILES
1 cup chocolate buttons
Grated pistachio or macadamia nuts
pinch of edible dried petals

METHOD

Melt butter and dark chocolate together. You will need to break the chocolate into pieces, of course, to help it melt easier. Once melted stir through until smooth and allow to cool slightly. Beat eggs and castor sugar together until pale and fluffy.

Sift plain flour, baking powder, Ras el Hanout, and cocoa powder together. Mix all of these together to make a smooth batter, and also add chocolate chips or roasted nuts of your choice.

Spoon into a greased baking sheet and then bake in a moderate oven of 180c for 20-25 minutes until firm on the outside but still very gooey on the inside…do not be tempted to overcook these; they are best when extremely gooey.

CHOCOLATE TILES

Melt the chocolate for 1 minute in the microwave until melted and stir until smooth. Use a spatula to 'paint' the melted chocolate onto a greased silicone mat or baking mat. Paint out until nice and even, to about an A4 size, decorate with the grated nut dust and the petals, and allow to set in the fridge or if cool enough, on the counter. cut into squares and used to decorate houses.

1-2 sheets filo pastry brushed with melted butter, cut into perfect squares, then baked in an oven of 180c until brown and crunchy. Cool, and then use it to finish off your brownie house.

Chocolate Ganache

SERVINGS:

INGREDIENTS

500g chocolate buttons or diced chocolate
250ml cream
Cacao to dust

METHOD

Heat the cream until it boils through once. Add the chocolate and stir through; the residual heat should be enough to melt the chocolate.

When cool, place into a piping bag and leave to set a little, maybe for an hour. After an hour, pipe small dollops onto a tray dusted with cocoa. Shake around a little bit to coat and then shape into a ball using your hands to roll them.

Set in fridge-remove from the fridge and place in a container with sieved cacao powder in shake and store in an air-tight container in the fridge or freezer - can be used to decorate cakes.

TO SERVE

Serve as per presentation, with fresh berries and flower petals - gorgeous and SO versatile!

Complexion-Busting Chocolate Salami

SERVINGS: 6-8

INGREDIENTS

200g good quality chocolate (75% cocoa)
100ml coconut cream
1/2 cup toasted coconut, shredded
1/2 cup toasted cashews (unsalted)
1/2 cup pistachios or other nuts; almonds are cheaper
1/2 cup dates or dried fruit
1 teaspoon vanilla bean paste
Nuts, biscotti or toasted coconut, ground to a 'dust'

METHOD

Melt the chocolate in the microwave for about 1 minute until it has softened, and you can stir it into a smooth paste. Do not overcook your chocolate. Add the remaining ingredients and place on a piece of parchment paper, then roll up as a 'salami', coating it in either nut dust, biscotti dust or coconut, and then chill before slicing or even rolling into 'goodie' balls… check your skin for a healthy glow soon after eating these!

Death by Chocolate Complexion Busting Pistachio Rocky Road

SERVINGS:

INGREDIENTS

200g 75% good quality chocolate

100ml coconut cream

½ cup toasted coconut shredded

½ cup toasted cashews

½ cup pistachios or other nuts, almonds are cheaper

½ cup dates or dried fruit

1 teaspoon vanilla bean paste

METHOD

Melt the chocolate in the microwave for about 1 minute until you can stir it smooth; add the remaining ingredients and then roll it up as a 'salami' in some greaseproof paper, rolling it to form a sausage or salami, coating it in either nut dust, biscotti dust or coconut and then chill before slicing or even rolling into 'goodie' balls. Check your skin for a healthy glow soon after eating these.

Chocolate Bark or Tiles

SERVINGS:

INGREDIENTS

1 cup chocolate buttons

METHOD

1 cup chocolate buttons melted in the microwave for one minute until just soft; stir through until smooth. Once smooth spread out onto a greased piece of paper or a plastic mat and spread out until nice and even and thin.

Now decorate with petals, honeycomb crumbs, and any other dessert dust.
Allow to set and then crack or cut up into tiles and use as beautiful decorations on all types of desserts.

Dessert Dust

SERVINGS:

INGREDIENTS

50 g chocolate curls

50 g freeze-dried berries or honeycomb

50g cookie crumbs

50g sugar glass (use spun sugar recipe but pour the caramel sugar onto a greased tray, cool and then crack)

METHOD

Simply mix these together for a sensational dessert dust to go over ice cream balls, or as presentation on your dessert plate!

Delectable Foams

ALL RECIPES MAKE 4 SERVINGS

Essentially, to break it down for you and give you a base for any foam to match any dish, you will need 1 egg white, 1 bloomed sheet of gelatin added just after the liquid is strained and still hot, and a pinch of cream of tartar TO 250ml liquid.

Beetroot & Rosemary Foam (savoury)

INGREDIENTS

2 tablespoons chopped beetroot fresh
1 teaspoon rosemary freshly chopped
250ml apple juice

METHOD

Boil together and then strain; add 1 sheet of bloomed leaf gelatin and cool. Now add 1 egg white and 1/8 teaspoon cream of tartar and stir. When cool, use your stick blender to whisk until lovely red foam is created!

Lime & Cilantro Foam (savoury)

INGREDIENTS

1 bunch coriander
1-teaspoon lime zest

METHOD

50ml lime juice boiled in 150 orange juice and 100 water and then blended to form a thick green 'sloshy' liquid.
Strain and then add 1 sheet of bloomed leaf gelatin and cool. Now add 1 egg white and 1/8 teaspoon cream of tartar and stir. When cool, use your stick blender to whisk until lovely green foam is created!

Strawberry, Lemon & Basil Foam (sweet)

INGREDIENTS

3 tablespoons sugar
3-5 strawberries diced
1 teaspoon fresh beetroot
(if you have some, will spike the red colour)
Zest and juice of 1 lemon 200ml water

METHOD

Boil until the sugar has dissolved, about 5 minutes. Then add 1 sheet bloomed leaf gelatin and cool.
Now add 1 egg white and 1/8 teaspoon cream of tartar and stir. When cool and use your stick blender to whisk until lovely red foam is created!

NOTES

NOTES

Meet Chef Mel
THE HAPPY CHEF

PASSIONATE FOODIE, AUTHOR, ENTREPRENEUR, COOKING SCHOOL TEACHER, ATHLETE, CULTURAL GASTRONOMER AND CHEF

With a smile that can light up a room, she has been dubbed "The Happy Chef" by her students. Chef Mel is brilliant at making everyday dishes dazzling.
Her clever approach to cooking and teaching focuses on making recipes easy to understand, with time spent on excellent presentation skills.

The enthusiastic, entertaining, award-winning African-Australian chef and cooking school owner says that with some know-how, anyone can plate up spectacular spreads like those you would expect to see in five-star restaurants.
Her intoxicating enthusiasm, authenticity and culinary lingo will have you hungry to flex your muscles in the kitchen.

She promises that this book will teach you some seriously cheffy skills so that you will be so much more confident and happy in your kitchen.

She can't wait to help you become the foodie you have always wanted to be.

Get ready to make delicious discoveries.